The Return of
Rudolf Steiner

and the

Renewal of Anthroposophy

RON MACFARLANE

Copyright © 2020 Ron MacFarlane

All rights reserved.

Published 2020 by
Greater Mysteries Publications
Mission, BC, Canada

Cover Design: Ron MacFarlane

Printed in the United States of America

ISBN:
ISBN-13: 978-0-9959674-2-7
ISBN-10: 0-9959674-0-3

DEDICATION

Eternal praise and honour
is hereby bestowed
on that magnanimous soul who,
in his Hellenistic incarnation as Aristotle,
single-handedly provided mankind
with the logical tools
to intellectually master the physical world.
Then, in his medieval incarnation as St. Thomas Aquinas,
he forged an intellectual path to Christ
for struggling humanity
by uniting Aristotelian philosophy with Catholic theology.
And in his last incarnation as Rudolf Steiner,
he sacrificially established
an authentic spiritual science
in order to lead the human intellect
back to the spiritual world.

The front and back covers are original designs by the author.

The background images on the front and back covers are from a painting of the Himalayas by Nicholas Roerich (1874–1947).

The foreground image on the back cover is a painting of the interior of Steiner's first, large architectural structure—the House of St. John—that was unfortunately destroyed by arson.

CONTENTS

THE
RETURN OF
RUDOLF STEINER

AND THE

RENEWAL OF

ANTHROPOSOPHY

"Every man is born an Aristotelian or a Platonist"

(Samuel Taylor Coleridge: 1830)

INTRODUCTION

THE PREMATURE DEATH in 1925 of Austrian philosopher and esotericist—Rudolf Steiner—at the age of 64, was a devastating "body-blow" to the newly-constituted General Anthroposophical Society and to its world-wide members.

Even though Steiner had been seriously ill, and often bed-ridden for six months prior to his death, everyone expected that this extraordinarily-gifted individual would fully recover. After all, Steiner was widely recognized as a highly-developed Christian initiate with demonstrated supernatural abilities.[1]

Besides that, throughout his worsening illness, Steiner himself talked and acted as though he expected to fully recover. Not only had he assumed the presidency of the Society and taken up the leadership of the School of Spiritual Science just nine months before becoming ill; but even after becoming seriously afflicted, he continued to dictate letters, to record new supersensible research, to work on his autobiography, to write weekly essays for the newsletter *Das Goetheanum*, and to provide personal counseling for a constant flow of members and non-members. Hardly the funerary activities of a man who was preparing to die.

The shock, surprise, disbelief and despair that

anthroposophists experienced with the death of Rudolf Steiner similarly echoed that of the apostles and disciples of Christ-Jesus immediately after his own premature death at 33 years of age. No one expected that the Messiah, with his demonstrated divine power, would be cruelly put to death by Roman execution (despite his repeated prophetic indications that this would occur).

In the case of Christ-Jesus, his unwavering compassion to rescue fallen humanity was placed far above personal concerns for his own physical safety. For this reason, he willingly sacrificed his own physical life despite the enormous spiritual power at his command. Nevertheless, notwithstanding his untimely death, he positively left behind the strong foundation for a future universal church, and the promise that he would one day return to earth.

In Rudolf Steiner's case, as a devoted follower of Christ-Jesus, he similarly minimized and disregarded the seriousness of his own physical health in order to compassionately continue to assist those around him, and to help struggling humanity in general. Unfortunately, this too resulted in his own sacrificial death. And similar to Our Saviour, Rudolf Steiner positively left behind the foundation for a world-wide esoteric society; and the indication that he would return to earth in less than a hundred years.

Also noteworthy in both cases—with Christ-Jesus and Rudolf Steiner—their predicted return to earth was not what was generally expected to occur; but something that was quite different in fact. While briefly touching on the unique earthly return of Christ-Jesus that occurred in the twentieth century, this publication—*The Return of Rudolf Steiner and the Renewal of Anthroposophy*—will focus on explaining and understanding the predicted return to earth of Rudolf Steiner that quietly (but profoundly) occurred at the beginning of the twenty-first century; and the positive impact this will have on future anthroposophy.

CHAPTER 1

A DEEPER UNDERSTANDING OF RUDOLF STEINER

1.1 Previous Significant Incarnations of Rudolf Steiner

IN ORDER TO better understand the exceptionality of Rudolf Steiner's return to earth at the beginning of the twenty-first century, it's necessary to better understand and appreciate the extraordinary individuality of Rudolf Steiner himself.

Right from his very first incarnation as a human being on planet earth, it was obvious that the individuality who later became Rudolf Steiner was no ordinary soul. When the bulk of humanity fell into physical materiality during the ancient Lemurian Age,[2] the soul of Rudolf Steiner continued to separately abide in the etheric realm.[3] Even throughout the great Atlantean Age, his pristine soul had no experience of physical incarnation. It was only during the Egypto-Babylonian cultural era of the current Post-Atlantean Age—around 3000 BC—that the soul of Rudolf Steiner physically incarnated on earth for the very first time.[4]

1.1.1 Steiner's First Earthly Incarnation as the Legendary Figure, <u>Enkidu</u>

Remarkably, Rudolf Steiner's very first incarnation has been historically recorded in an ancient Mesopotamian epic-poem entitled, *The Epic of Gilgamesh* (c.1800 BC). Enkidu, one of the principal figures mentioned in the poem, is based on Steiner's first physical embodiment. Even though the characters and events in this epic-poem have been mythologically embellished, it's still possible to deduce some historical accuracy regarding Steiner's incarnation as Enkidu.

For example, Enkidu is described as a "wild man" who lived among the animals, and who had an innate affinity with the natural world around him. This description accurately indicates the esoteric fact that since Enkidu had no prior incarnations, his nascent soul would've had no direct experience with human civilization or with cultural developments. Consequently, he would have initially retained a primordial oneness with nature that had diminished in most of "civilized" mankind.

In addition, Enkidu is described in the poem as being a creation of the gods, who was placed on earth in order to end the tyrannical rule of Gilgamesh, king of Uruk. Since Enkidu had no prior incarnations, his long sojourn in the etheric realm since ancient Lemuria would require the protection and direction of higher spiritual beings; particularly the sun-god, or "Christ-Spirit" (called "Shamash" in the *Epic*). As well, even though he etherically existed *above* the physical world, Enkidu was obviously not *detached* from human affairs on earth. In order to deal with a powerful king during his very first incarnation, Enkidu would obviously have needed some adequate preparation prior to birth.

According to *The Epic*, Enkidu lost his innate

"wildness"—his inborn oneness with nature—through the seduction of an Ishtar priestess who was sent by Gilgamesh to corrupt him. Thereafter, Enkidu became "civilized"; he learned social manners, spoken language, occupational skills and worldly knowledge. No doubt, these story-details accurately indicate how Enkidu was understandably seduced by the pleasures of the physical world, and how these temptations impaired the cosmic oneness of his previously-virgin soul.

Despite their initial antagonism, *The Epic* then goes on to relate how Enkidu and Gilgamesh became close friends[5] uniting their powers to defeat some powerful supernatural foes, and to share a fateful "journey to the underworld." Esotericists understand that this phrase means that both men were initiated in one of the secretive, Middle-Eastern Mystery centres.[6]

Unfortunately, according to *The Epic* story, Enkidu remained trapped in the underworld during his initiatory journey, which resulted in his death. Historically speaking, death was not uncommon during Mystery initiation, since the candidate was placed in a dangerous trance-like condition for three full days. Nevertheless, the discarnate soul (the "shade") of Enkidu was able to escape the underworld, and to communicate some of his acquired supernatural knowledge to his friend Gilgamesh.[7]

From the mythological details of *The Epic of Gilgamesh*, it is clearly obvious that Rudolf Steiner's first earthly incarnation as Enkidu indicates that he was already a highly-advanced and exceptional individuality.

1.1.2 Steiner's Next Significant Incarnation as the Ancient Greek Philosopher, <u>Cratylus</u>

Rudolf Steiner's next noteworthy incarnation was during the Graeco-Roman cultural era as the Greek philosopher

Cratylus (mid-late 5th century BC). Cratylus was known to be a pupil of influential mystic-philosopher, Heraclitus (c.535–c.475 BC); and is credited with introducing the famous philosopher, Plato (c.429–347 BC.), with the penetrating ideas of Heraclitus—such as that of the Logos being the principle of reason which underlies the universe.

With this particular incarnation, there is the first clear indication that the soul of Rudolf Steiner has been repeatedly involved in crucially–pivotal events in human history. In regard to the critical nature of ancient Greek civilization, one of the outstanding cultural characteristics was a predominant emphasis on artistic beauty—finely-painted pottery; colourfully-large mosaics; superbly-crafted jewelry and metalwork; stunningly-beautiful bas-relief and freestanding sculpture; breathtaking temple architecture; and realistic wall and fresco painting.

Unfortunately during this time, Lucifer was deliberately intensifying artistic sentiment and sensual pleasure in a covert attempt to seductively divert human interest and attention away from the harsh realities of the physical world. Since the very inception of human selfhood during the ancient Lemurian Age, Lucifer's unrealized goal has been to materialize and control a bogus planet within the solar system; and then to illicitly populate it with somnolent human souls enticed away from the earth.[8]

To counteract and prevent this dangerous luciferic enticement, the benevolent spiritual beings who guide human evolution inspired the intellectual development of Greek philosophy. The power of deep intellectual thought that was initiated by Heraclitus and promulgated by Steiner's incarnation as Cratylus was critically necessary to preserve progressive human development on earth during that time.[9]

1.1.3 Steiner's World-Altering Incarnation as <u>Aristotle</u>

According to esoteric research, the usual length of time for deceased souls between incarnations is several hundred years. So, when the soul of Rudolf Steiner re-embodied in ancient Greece after less than a hundred years, this once again demonstrated his extraordinary spiritual attainment. Furthermore, it's astounding to discover that as Cratylus, the soul of Rudolf Steiner was a *teacher* of Plato, and in his very next incarnation as Aristotle (384–322 BC), he was a *pupil* of Plato. It is also esoterically significant that during the time the young Aristotle attended Plato's Academy in Athens, he was very likely initiated into the sacred Mysteries of Eleusis (which was only about 11 miles from Athens).

Aristotle has been esteemed throughout history for his towering and sweeping intellect which made significant contributions to physics, mathematics, metaphysics, biology, botany, agriculture, medicine, politics, dance, theatre and ethics. But it was his completely-original, entirely-unprecedented, single-handed development of the method and practice of logical reasoning that would forever change the course of human history.

Prior to Aristotle, ancient Greek philosophers were primarily interested in intellectually generating and employing concepts and ideas in the mind. Aristotle was really the first thinker to intellectually examine the inner workings of the mind itself, and not simply the cognitive products of the mind. By formulating the rules of deductive logic, Aristotle provided human beings with a reliable method of acquiring knowledge of the sensory, natural world.

This of course placed him at ideological odds with the philosophy of his illustrious teacher, Plato. According to Platonic philosophy, the world of the senses was imperfect and unreliable since it was constantly changing. Consequently, eternal, unchanging truth and reality was only to be found in the spirit-filled ideas and forms (or "archetypes") that existed at the transcendent level of universal mind (the Logos).

In contrast, according to Aristotelian philosophy, archetypal ideas and forms were pervasively ingenerated throughout the sensory, material world. By employing deductive logic and reasoning, it was possible to discover immutable, universal truth by studying the sensory, material world.

Not surprisingly, then, Platonists correctly blamed the rise of natural science and humanity's continued descent into physical materiality on Aristotelian philosophy. Aristotelians, on the other hand, believed that positive, evolutionary development necessitated that mankind gain mastery of the physical world; and not simply to disregard or ignore it. Unfortunately, this philosophical animosity was to continue down through the centuries until the late-twentieth century.[10]

Also historically noteworthy regarding Steiner's incarnation as Aristotle is the fact that (at the request of King Philip II of Macedon) he acted as tutor for Alexander the Great between the ages of thirteen and sixteen. Since Aristotle planted the notion of "eastern conquest" in the mind of young Alexander, in this way he contributed to the spread of Greek culture and civilization throughout the Middle East, western India and northern Egypt.

Very much like his incarnation as Rudolf Steiner,[11] Aristotle was a prolific writer and lecturer. He produced many hundreds of books on papyrus scrolls, and also wrote many elegant treatises and dialogues which he stored in a library that he established in the Athenian Lyceum. Unfortunately, only about a third of his original writings have survived.

1.1.4 Steiner's Incarnation as <u>Schionatulander</u>: A Knight of the Holy Grail

During the life of Christ-Jesus on earth, the soul of Rudolf Steiner was not in physical incarnation; but was active in the superphysical realms of existence. Early in the Christian Age, during the time of Charlemagne (748–814), the soul of Rudolf Steiner incarnated as a knight of the Holy Grail; known to legend as Schionatulander.[12] The figure of Schionatulander was mentioned in two, popular, medieval epic-poems: the first was by twelfth-century French poet, Chrétien de Troyes, entitled *Perceval, the Story of the Grail*; and the second was by a famous German poet-knight, Wolfram von Eschenbach (c.1160–c.1220), entitled *Parzival*.

Unfortunately, the details of Schionatulander's life in both epic-poems are confusing, conflicting and unreliable. Moreover, both poets muddle the figures and events of the Knights of the Round Table with the figures and events of the Knights of the Holy Grail. King Arthur's Round Table was a secret, pre-Christian Mystery brotherhood that was centred in ancient Wales. The Grail Knights, on the other hand, were a secret, medieval Christian brotherhood that was centred in northern Spain.

Nevertheless, the central significance of Steiner's medieval life as Schionatulander is that his very first important incarnation during the Christian Age was within the Johannine stream of esoteric Christianity. This was certainly a logical progression since the immortal soul of Rudolf Steiner had been repeatedly initiated in various ancient Mysteries; and since throughout antiquity he had been under the guidance and protection of the exalted sun-god (the "Christ-Spirit").

By incarnating as a knight of the Holy Grail, the medieval soul of Rudolf Steiner endeavoured to more deeply comprehend the supernatural life and salvational mission of Christ-Jesus. Once again, in close association with Steiner during this time, was the soul of Ita Wegman, who incarnated as Sigûne, the Grail figure tragically betrothed to Schionatulander.

Another very important esoteric figure who was also incarnated at this time was the Grail knight, Parsifal.

Esotericists recognize that the soul of Parsifal was a very highly-advanced Christian initiate; who, as Mani (c.216–c.277) in a previous incarnation, founded the once-popular Persian religion of Manichaeism.[13] A central concept of Manichaeism is the cosmological battle of good and evil; so in this respect the soul of Parsifal (aided by that of Rudolf Steiner) was well-suited to combat the forces of black magic that were aimed at destroying the Knights of the Holy Grail.[14]

Schionatulander's association with Parsifal in this incarnation is another clear indication that the soul of Rudolf Steiner moved among some very illustrious and mutually-extraordinary individuals throughout his major incarnations.

1.1.5 Steiner's Influential Incarnation as St. Thomas Aquinas, the Preeminent "Doctor of the Church."

Even though St. John the evangelist established the path of esoteric Christianity (such as the search for the Holy Grail), he also contributed to the path of exoteric Christianity (the Church of St. Peter). The Gospel of John has historically served as an initiatory guide-book for the Mystic-Christianity that was practiced within the various monastic orders of the Church. Similarly, even though the soul of Rudolf Steiner contributed to the Johannine stream of esoteric Christianity during his incarnation as the Grail knight, Schionatulander, in his subsequent incarnation as St. Thomas Aquinas (1225–1274), he immensely contributed to the stream of exoteric Christianity.

During his incarnation in ancient Greece as the philosopher Aristotle, the soul of Rudolf Steiner—by directing his immense intellectual attention to the sensory, physical world—provided humanity with a new avenue of acquiring knowledge and understanding of the world.

Even though he continued to argue for the importance and value of the natural world of the senses, St. Thomas also directed his own prodigious intellectual prowess[15] to understanding spiritual matters; particularly the reality of Christ-Jesus and his salvational work for mankind. To assist in this intellectual endeavor, he superbly combined Aristotelian philosophy with Christian theology.[16] In doing so, St. Thomas began to intellectually direct mankind's attention back to the spiritual world without deprecating the sensory, physical world.[17]

Even though the medieval knights of the Holy Grail attained a far-deeper supernatural understanding of Christ-Jesus' sacrificial death on the cross (known esoterically as the "Mystery of Golgotha") than did the medieval Church of St. Peter, they were still unable to express and convey this spirit-wisdom in clear intellectual concepts. Consequently, their esoteric knowledge was conveyed through ritual enactments, dramatic performances, artistic symbolism, and legendary stories. The Grail chalice itself—the communion cup of the Last Supper which supposedly collected the shed blood of Christ-Jesus on the cross—functioned as the symbolic receptacle for the esoteric-wisdom of Christ-Jesus.

It took St. Thomas' genius of uniting Aristotelian philosophy with Church theology to understand the mystery of Holy Communion in clear intellectual concepts for the very first time. This in turn shed intellectual light on the mystery of the Holy Grail.

The deep mystery of Our Saviour's "real presence" in the sacrament of Holy Communion began at the Last Supper when he declared:

> Now as they were eating, Jesus took bread, and blessed, and broke it, and gave it to the disciples and said, "Take, eat; this is my body." And he took a cup, and when he had given thanks he gave it to them, saying, "Drink of it, all of you; for this is my blood of the covenant, which is poured out for many for the forgiveness of sins. (Matt 26:26–28)

Regarding the sacramental bread and wine, since Christ-Jesus definitively declared that the bread *is* his body, and the wine *is* his blood, the Church of St. Peter has always believed that Christ-Jesus is truly present in Holy Communion. Our Saviour did not say that the consecrated bread and wine "represented" his body and blood, or were mere "symbols" of his body and blood.

Nevertheless, as to how Christ-Jesus miraculously becomes present in the sacramental bread and wine was regarded as a supreme mystery of the Church that had to be accepted on faith—a *mysterium fidei*. A number of terms was used by the early Church to describe this mystery of mysteries: "change," "becomes," "alteration," "transposing," "transformation," and "transelementation."

By 1215, at the Fourth Council of the Lateran, the term "transubstantiation" became the preferred term, though there was no attempt at that time to intellectually explain the term. Soon after the Council, St. Thomas provided some satisfactory conceptual clarity by applying Aristotle's explanation of sense-perceptible reality.

According to Aristotle, all reality was divisible into two distinctions, which he termed: (1) "substances," and (2) "accidents." Both terms have a specific philosophical use that differs from their everyday usage. "Substance" in this case doesn't mean chemical elements; but rather the defining essence of a person or thing (a combination of form and matter). Accidents in this case doesn't mean unintended harmful events; but rather, the descriptive features of a substance (such as colour, shape or weight). Philosophically, a substance exists *in itself*; whereas an accident exists *in a substance* but not in itself.

Applying Aristotle's ideas to the Eucharistic bread and wine, St. Thomas elegantly explained that during the ritual sacrament of the Church, the substances of the bread and wine were "transubstantiated" into the substances of Christ-

Jesus' body and blood—but the accidents remained the same. In other words, after the transubstantiation, the bread and wine looked exactly the same as to taste, colour, size, weight, texture, and so on; but the underlying essence of the "things in themselves"—the substances—were now the body and blood of Christ-Jesus.

Even more correctly, since a living body with blood can't logically exist without a soul and divinity, the transubstantiated substance of both the bread and the wine was the "real presence," the entire person—body, blood, soul and divinity—of Christ-Jesus. As stated in the *Compendium: Catechism of the Catholic Church* (2006):

> Jesus Christ is present in the Eucharist in a unique and incomparable way. He is present in a true, real and substantial way, with his Body and his Blood, with his Soul and his Divinity. In the Eucharist, therefore, there is present in a sacramental way, that is, under the Eucharistic species of bread and wine, Christ whole and entire, God and Man. (Paragraph 282)

Therefore, when the transubstantiated bread and wine of Holy Communion are ingested, the partaker is intimately united with the entire person of Christ-Jesus.

Even though St. Thomas had managed to provide some satisfactory intellectual understanding of the mystery of Holy Communion (and by extension, the mystery of the Holy Grail), at first he wasn't entirely happy with his initial explanatory efforts. As described by G. K. Chesterton in *St. Thomas Aquinas* (2012):

> When he was stationed at Paris, the other Doctors of the Sorbonne put before him a problem about the nature of the mystical change in the elements of the Blessed Sacrament, and he proceeded to write, in his customary manner, a very careful and elaborately lucid statement of his own solution. Needless to say he felt with hearty

simplicity the heavy responsibility and gravity of such a judicial decision; and not unnaturally seems to have worried about it more than he commonly did over his work. He sought for guidance in more than usually prolonged prayer and intercession; and finally, with one of those few but striking bodily gestures that mark the turning points of his life, he threw down his thesis at the foot of the crucifix on the altar, and left it lying there; as if awaiting judgment. Then he turned and came down the altar steps and buried himself once more in prayer; but the other Friars, it is said, were watching; and well they might be. For they declared afterwards that the figure of Christ had come down from the cross before their mortal eyes; and stood upon the scroll, saying "Thomas, thou hast written well concerning the Sacrament of My Body." It was after this vision that the incident is said to have happened, of his being born up miraculously in mid-air.

This particular incident is one noteworthy demonstration that St. Thomas possessed more than just unsurpassed intellectual capacity; he also exhibited profound clairvoyant perception and advanced supernatural ability. In one instance, St. Paul appeared to Thomas in order to assist him with a difficult piece of writing. In another instance the Blessed Virgin Mary comfortingly appeared to him with the welcome news that he would never be a bishop. There were also many well-attested instances of St. Thomas levitating in ecstasy while in prayer.

The best known of St. Thomas' supernatural events occurred in 1273, just a year before he died. In a Dominican convent in Naples, he was observed tearfully levitating in prayer before an icon of the crucified Christ. Whereupon, Christ is purported to have said, "You have written well of me, Thomas. What reward would you have for your labor?" St. Thomas is said to have replied, "Nothing but you, Lord."

While St. Thomas was always reluctant to discuss his

supernatural experiences, he later shared with his secretary and confessor, Reginald of Piperno[18] (c. 1230–c.1290), that he had received a vision of such transcendence that all his previous writings "seemed like straw." As a result, St. Thomas discontinued to write up until his death three months later. Since this particular "heavenly" experience occurred so close to his death, no doubt it was a pre-vision of his life after death, and a foretaste of the remarkable clairvoyant insight that the soul of St. Thomas would possess in his next illustrious incarnation as Rudolf Steiner.

1.2 Rudolf Steiner: The Saviour of Intellectual Thought

For those who acknowledge the profound contribution that Rudolf Steiner has made for present and future human development, it's disconcerting to learn that he almost didn't incarnate on February 25, 1861, in the village of Kraljevec. Soon after birth, severe hemorrhaging occurred due to poorly-applied navel bandaging performed by the midwife. Fearing that the infant may not survive, the distraught parents, Johann and Franziska, arranged for an emergency baptism in nearby Draskovec.[19] Two days later, on February 27, Rudolf Joseph Lorenz Steiner was baptized into the Catholic Church.[20]

1.2.1 Steiner's Karmic Connection with the Catholic Church

Esoterically speaking, it's rather fitting that Rudolf Steiner entered into this world as a Catholic, since he left this world as a devoted Catholic in his previous incarnation as St. Thomas Aquinas. In a very real sense, as Rudolf Steiner, he was destined to continue and further advance the brilliant work that he had established as St. Thomas Aquinas.

It should come as no surprise, then, that the sensitive soul of the young, eight-year-old Rudolf Steiner was so deeply moved by the sacred rituals of the Holy Mass that he decided to become an altar-server for the parish church in Neudörfl. Noteworthy as well, this firm, youthful decision was entirely his own initiative; since his father Johann was a staunch non-practicing Catholic at that time, and a vocal critic of the Austrian clergy. As Rudolf Steiner himself later explained in his unfinished autobiography, *The Course of My Life* (1986):

> The solemnity of the Latin language and of the liturgy was a thing in which my boyish soul found a vital happiness …

> Out of my boyhood at Neudörfl I have the strongest impression of the way in which the contemplation of the rites of the church, in connection with the solemnity of liturgical music, causes the riddles of existence to rise in powerful suggestive fashion before the mind. The instruction in the Bible and the catechism imparted by the priest had far less effect upon my inner world than what he accomplished as celebrant of the cultus in mediating between the sensible and the supersensible world. From the first, all this was to me no mere form, but a profound experience.

It's certainly no secret that during his life Rudolf Steiner was openly critical of the ultra-orthodox Jesuit influence in the Catholic Church of the early-twentieth century. Nevertheless, in a lecture he gave in 1924, he made the startling (to some) admission that as a teenager he almost joined the Cistercian Order of the Catholic Church. He attributed this to the fact that his father sent him to the "realschule" in Wiener-Neustadt rather than the "gymnasium" to be educated. Since the humanities courses in the gymnasiums were often taught by Cistercians, Steiner maintained that if he had attended the gymnasium instead of the realschule he would have certainly become a Cistercian priest. As he himself stated:

> I was deeply attracted to all these [Cistercian] priests, many of whom were extremely learned men. I read a great deal that they wrote and was profoundly stirred by it. I loved these priests and the only reason why I passed the Cistercian Order by was because I did not attend the Gymnasium. Karma led me elsewhere. (Lecture given on "The Karma of the Anthroposophical Society"; 18 June 1924)

Once again, there is a definite karmic connection between Rudolf Steiner and his previous incarnation as St. Thomas Aquinas. Even though St. Thomas was a lifelong and devoted member of the Dominican Order, his final days were gratefully spent under the tender care of the Cistercian monks at the Abbey of Fossanova. As St. Thomas shared with Reginald, his confessor: "This is my rest for ever and ever: here will I dwell, for I have chosen it" (Psalm 131:14).

1.2.2 Steiner's Karmic Continuation of his Philosophical Mission for Humanity

In the case of most healthy fourteen-year-old boys, it would seem rather extraordinary for them to take an interest in reading German philosopher Immanuel Kant's (1724–1804) *Critique of Pure Reason* (1781). But in Rudolf Steiner's case, not only was he interested—he was actually excited about reading it. As he described in his autobiography:

> My boundless interest in the *Critique of Pure Reason* had arisen entirely out of my own mental life. In my boyish way, I was striving to understand what human reason might be able to achieve toward a real insight into the

nature of things. (*The Course of My Life*; 1986)

Of course, this comes as no surprise to those who are familiar with Rudolf Steiner's previous incarnations. In three of them—as Cratylus, Aristotle and St. Thomas Aquinas—the immortal soul of Rudolf Steiner was engaged in philosophical intellection that profoundly altered human civilization. Quite naturally, then, the adolescent Rudolf Steiner was karmically driven to assimilate all the major philosophical thinking that had occurred since his last incarnation as St. Thomas Aquinas.

Consequently, the young Rudolf Steiner set about studying and absorbing the philosophy of Johann Herbart (1776–1841), Johann Fichte (1762–1814), Friedrich Schelling (1775–1854), Georg Hegel (1770–1831), Franz Brentano (1838–1917), Arthur Schopenhauer (1788–1860) and Eduard von Hartmann (1842–1906). As Steiner himself described in his autobiography:

> My first visit to Vienna after we moved to Inzersdorf was used for the purpose of buying a greater number of philosophical books ...

> The summer months of 1879 [when I was 18], from the end of my *Realschule* course until my entrance into the *Technische Hochschule,* I spent entirely in such philosophical studies. (Ibid)

It's rather remarkable that the adolescent Rudolf Steiner was able to devote such time and energy into such seriously-comprehensive philosophical study considering that his onerous course-work at the realschule and Technische Hochschule was in science, mathematics, geometry and engineering. Thankfully, the abstract, non-sensory nature of mathematical thinking positively contributed to young Steiner's spiritual understanding of pure thought; stated as follows:

Mathematics retained its importance for me as the foundation also of my striving after knowledge. For mathematics provides a system of percepts and concepts which have been arrived at independently of any external sense-impression. (Ibid)

Equally remarkable during young Steiner's formative educational years is the recognition that he was not just assimilating the significant knowledge that mankind had acquired since his incarnation as St. Thomas Aquinas; but that he was also formulating an entirely new and original understanding of intellectual thinking itself. As he himself stated:

It was no light matter for my mental life at that time that the philosophy which I learned from others could not in its thinking be carried all the way to the perception of the spiritual world. Out of the difficulties which I experienced in this respect, a kind of "theory of knowledge" began to take form within me. (Ibid)

The nineteen-year-old Rudolf Steiner realized that he was alone in his philosophical belief that knowledge of the spiritual world could be accurately acquired through intellectual reasoning—that is, until he discovered Johann von Goethe (1749–1832). Young Steiner was introduced to the highly-influential writings of Goethe through Karl Julius Schröer (1825–1900), a professor of German literature at the Hochschule.[21] In Goethe, Steiner found a kindred spirit—a respected philosopher who also experienced clairvoyant perceptions, and who endeavored to understand them with clear scientific reasoning.[22]

Even though Goethe's scientific writings encouraged and inspired the young Steiner, he still felt that Goethe hadn't completely understood the true nature of thinking. Consequently, Steiner's determination to formulate a new theory of knowledge eventually culminated in 1894 with the publication of *The Philosophy of Spiritual Activity.*[23]

With this publication, the 33-year old Steiner's understanding of intellectual thinking was a brilliantly-original departure from all that had been understood before. Previously, philosophers and scientists had argued that intellectual thinking was only capable of acquiring knowledge of the physical, sense-perceptible world. It was believed to be entirely incapable of acquiring knowledge of the spiritual world (if one actually existed).

In *The Philosophy of Spiritual Activity* Steiner revealed that pure cognition was a spiritual activity.[24] As such, not only is intellectual reasoning capable of acquiring knowledge of the spiritual world; but thinking itself can be directly experienced as an activity in the spiritual world.

What Rudolf Steiner momentously accomplished in the history of philosophy was the salvation of intellectual thinking. He freed human reasoning from the pernicious, materialistic notion that it was nothing but a physical, brain-based activity. He also freed intellectual thinking from being exclusively chained to the sense-perceptible natural world by revealing that the content of thinking can be spiritual as well as physical.

Esoterically understood, Rudolf Steiner karmically completed what he had begun as Aristotle. By developing the tools of logical reasoning to acquire knowledge of sense-perceptible nature, Aristotle directed mankind's intellectual attention to the physical world. As St. Thomas Aquinas, by philosophically arguing that "reason" was not incompatible with "faith" (the infallible truths of the Church), he laid the foundation for scientifically studying nature as a reliable method of gaining intellectual certainty of God's existence. Once again, he directed mankind's intellectual attention to sense-perceptible nature as a "worthy study" of God's universal creation. Then, as Rudolf Steiner, once mankind had gained sufficient knowledge of the physical world, he directed mankind's intellectual attention back to the spiritual world where it properly belongs.

1.2.3 Rudolf Steiner Establishes the First "Science of the Spirit"

Once Rudolf Steiner had formulated a new theory of knowledge that accurately corresponded with reality, it was predictable that soon afterward he would endeavor to establish a practical application of this discovery. Hence the esoteric foundation of the first authentic "science of the spirit" in human history.

Once again, Goethe can be credited with providing Steiner with the inspiration needed for such an undertaking, as indicated from the following:

> Goethe's way of conceiving nature becomes one which, by tracing the natural development from the inorganic to the organic, leads natural science over into a spiritual science. (Rudolf Steiner; Ibid)

In addition to postulating the superphysical nature of pure intellectual thought that can be used to gather knowledge of the spiritual world, Rudolf Steiner's science of the spirit is also founded on the esoteric premise that human beings possesses innate, largely-undeveloped superphysical (soul) senses that can also be used to gather knowledge of the spiritual world. In the same way that empirical science uses the five physical senses and stringent intellectual reasoning to acquire knowledge of the natural world; spiritual science uses properly-developed, superphysical sense-perception—and the same sound scientific reasoning—to acquire knowledge of the supernatural world.

In this respect, Rudolf Steiner was ideally-placed to establish the first science of the spirit since—as a highly-advanced Christian initiate—he possessed preeminent supersensible perception. The depth and breadth of Steiner's spiritual-scientific research is truly breathtaking; with enough spiritual discoveries to provide scientific study for several centuries to come.

Rudolf Steiner named his new science of the spirit, "anthroposophy"; meaning the "spiritual wisdom of mankind." Not surprisingly, it took several years of growth and struggle for nascent anthroposophy to become a fully-established, clearly-defined spiritual science.

The first germination of anthroposophy was under the esoteric umbrella of the Theosophical Society,[25] when Rudolf Steiner became the secretary of the German Section in 1902. From the very beginning, Steiner presented Theosophical members with his own independently-researched, spiritual-scientific investigations that were free from any external influence (even from the Society).

For the first few years, Steiner referred to the accumulation of his own spiritual-scientific knowledge as "theosophy"; meaning the "wisdom of God." It was only after he split the German Section away from the Theosophical Society in 1907 that "theosophy" was replaced with "anthroposophy" as the term to describe his spiritual-scientific research.

As interest in Steiner's anthroposophical spiritual science increased and expanded throughout Europe during the early 1900s, this resulted in "anthroposophy" becoming an esoteric movement as well. When, in 1912, the Anthroposophical Society was founded, the term "anthroposophy" then came to refer to three distinct things: (1) spiritual science itself, (2) the social movement engendered by spiritual science, and (3) the society established to promote spiritual science.

In 1923-24, at what was called the "Christmas Conference," in order to resolve serious internal dissention among various members, Rudolf Steiner wisely decided to unify the three distinct elements of spiritual science into one overarching organization, the General Anthroposophical Society; with himself as the first president. Within the Society, Steiner also founded a School of Spiritual Science; and began construction on a new building—the Goetheanum—to house the new school, and to function as headquarters for the new Society. Henceforth, everything connected to anthroposophy has been united under the auspices of the General Anthroposophical Society.

1.3 Rudolf Steiner as Independent, Rosicrucian Initiate

Soon after he had discovered the influential writings of Johann von Goethe, the eighteen-year-old Steiner struck up a friendship on the train into Vienna with a middle-aged herb-gatherer named Felix Koguzki (1833–1906). Koguzki, who sold his herbs to various pharmacies in Vienna, possessed clairvoyant insight into the healing properties of various plants.

As well as being the first individual that the young Steiner met in life who also possessed supersensible perception, Koguzki, as a "secret messenger," introduced Steiner to a mysterious figure originally referred to as 'the M' (that is, "the Master"). Of course, these were no mere chance encounters; but highly-charged and significant karmic connections. The common esoteric thread that connected young Steiner to Goethe, to Koguzki, to the Master—was Rosicrucianism.

Through the enlightened writings of Goethe, young Steiner discovered a fellow scientific-philosopher who was familiar with the Rosicrucian Fraternity; and who incorporated Rosicrucian wisdom into his writing. This is particularly evident in the unfinished poem, *The Mysteries,*[26] and in the well-known fairy tale, *The Green Snake and the Beautiful Lily.*

With Felix Koguzki, young Steiner encountered and befriended an actual emissary of the Rosicrucian Fraternity. And with his subsequent secret-liaison with the Master, young Steiner encountered the actual physical incarnation of Christian Rosenkreutz—"Master CRC"—the illustrious founder of the Rosicrucian Fraternity.[27]

During this significant initial encounter, the Rosicrucian Master revealed to the eighteen-year-old Steiner that one of his life's missions was to overcome the materialistic spirit of the nineteenth century. In order to accomplish this, the Master is quoted as saying:

> To overcome the enemy, you must begin by understanding him. You can only become the conqueror of the dragon by slipping into his skin.[28]

Since it has been a strict traditional policy of the Rosicrucians to not publically reveal their secret identities in the Fraternity, Rudolf Steiner never openly declared that he was a Rosicrucian, or that 'the M' was Christian Rosenkreutz. Nevertheless, it's quite easy to infer that this was indeed the case. In Steiner's case, for instance, he gave hundreds of lectures that have been collected in dozens of books, that demonstrate a virtual torrent of deep Rosicrucian wisdom that was publically revealed for the first time in human history.[29]

Obviously, then, Rudolf Steiner had full access to the hidden treasure-house of Rosicrucian knowledge; and would not have had this access without being a Rosicrucian himself, or without the special permission of Christian Rosenkreutz. As with his unhindered relationship within the Theosophical Society, one can also surmise that Steiner had a similar free and independent relationship within the Rosicrucian Fraternity. It was important to Steiner, that in order to establish a true spiritual science, he required the freedom to supersensible verify all previously-held spirit-knowledge, including that retained by the Rosicrucian Fraternity.

As to the identity of 'the M' being Christian Rosenkreutz, well-informed anthroposophists are aware that Christian Rosenkreutz and the Master Zarathas are the advanced beings responsible for the spiritual development of Western societies, including those in Europe. It logically follows, then, that when the young Rudolf Steiner encountered an illustrious Master in the vicinity of Vienna, it would almost certainly be one of the two Masters responsible for Europe. Moreover, since Rudolf Steiner subsequently gained unprecedented access to Rosicrucian wisdom, as well as the freedom to publically divulge a wealth of this previously-guarded spiritual knowledge, this strongly suggests that 'the M' was indeed Christian Rosenkreutz.

1.4 Rudolf Steiner as One of the Twelve Bodhisattvas[30]

From the very beginning of his spiritual-scientific lecturing, Rudolf Steiner was immediately recognized as an incredibly-gifted esotericist and advanced-initiate. Predictably soon afterward, there was some quiet speculation that he was the Bodhisattva-Maitreya, the buddha of the future. Unfortunately, this faulty notion should have been easily refuted from the very start.

For one, the Bodhisattva-Maitreya is esoterically known to have previously incarnated in the first-century BC as the highly-respected Essene teacher—Yeshua ben Pandira. This was not one of Rudolf Steiner's previous lives. Even more convincingly, Steiner himself unequivocally denied that he and Maitreya were one and the same individuality. According to anthroposophic stenographer, Walter Vegelahn (1800–1959), Steiner made the following remarks at a meeting in 1910:

I wish to add in parenthesis to all those, who are ever ready to invent incarnations from their fantasy, that in my own individuality I have no connection with Jeshu ben Pandira.

Nevertheless, by acknowledging the world-altering impact of Rudolf Steiner's extraordinary incarnations, and from certain clairvoyant indications given by Steiner himself, one can confidently conclude that he was indeed a preeminent bodhisattva; but not Maitreya. Obviously Steiner's momentous contribution to the positive development of human intellectual reasoning over numerous lifetimes could only be accomplished by a supremely-advanced human being—such as a bodhisattva.

According to esoteric understanding, there exist twelve bodhisattva-beings who surround and serve the saviour of the world—Christ-Jesus. Though human, each has singularly advanced to the functioning-level of an archangel. Their varied responsibilities include the spiritual, cultural and material welfare of humanity throughout the ages. When not in physical incarnation, they operate from the etheric realm of Shambhala.

The clearest indication by Rudolf Steiner that he was a bodhisattva-being was given to intimate confidant, Ita Wegman, shortly after the Christmas Conference of 1923-24. Responding to her question about his relationship to Christian Rosenkreutz, Steiner presented Wegman with the following supersensible Imagination:

> One should think of oneself in a white garment, walking towards the altar, CR [Christian Rosenkreutz] with a blue stole standing on the left, RS [Rudolf Steiner] with a red stole standing to the right. One must think of this altar in the spiritual world.

This imagination clearly indicates that Rudolf Steiner was of equal and complementary spiritual-stature to Christian

Rosenkreutz. Since it is well-known by theosophists and anthroposophists that Christian Rosenkreutz is one of the twelve bodhisattvas, one can confidently conclude that Rudolf Steiner is one as well.

Acknowledging Rudolf Steiner's inclusion, the following is a tentative list of the twelve bodhisattvas:

(1) Christian Rosenkreutz (Master CRC)
(2) Zarathas (Master Jesus)
(3) Rudolf Steiner (Master RS)
(4) Lord Maitreya
(5) Manes (Manu)
(6) Kuthumi (Master KH)
(7) El Morya (Master M)
(8) Serapis (Skythianos)
(9) Hilarion (Master H)
(10) Paul the Venetian (The Venetian Master)
(11) The Maha Chohan
(12) Sanat Kumara

Given that Rudolf Steiner is a bodhisattva-being—an extraordinary individual—it naturally follows that his death was also an extraordinary event with extraordinary after-effects. This will be examined in greater detail in the following chapter.

CHAPTER 2

THE REPLICATION AND INTEGRATION OF STEINER'S AFTER-DEATH VEHICLES

2.1 The Principle of Spiritual Economy and Vehicles of Expression in Ancient Times

AS THE UNIVERSE continues to unfold and evolve, it has often taken vast stretches of time to refine and perfect particular forms and beings—from atoms to galaxies, and from bacteria to seraphim. Once something has reached an advanced stage of development, the forces of evolution endeavor to retain and replicate these progressive successes in order to elevate and enhance further evolution. This evolutionary process is esoterically known as the "principle of spiritual economy."

Since the spirit of God exists in eternity, it naturally follows that the more spiritualized a particular formation is within the universe, the more timeless and long-lasting it becomes. This of course includes the creations and accomplishments of highly-advanced individuals. A painting by Raphael (1483–1520) or a sculpture by Michelangelo

(1475–1654), for instance, both have a timeless, long-lasting quality since they are each suffused with transcendent spiritual thoughts and emotions.

Few esotericists are aware that the principle of spiritual economy also applies to the vehicles of expression—the etheric body, the astral body, soul vehicles and ego-bearing vehicle—of highly-advanced individuals; particularly avatars[31] and bodhisattva-beings. Normally when an individual dies, their various vehicles of expression are cast off in succession and slowly dissipate into their respective cosmic realms as the immortal spirit-self journeys heavenward to prepare for future rebirth. (Please refer to Figure 1 on page 30 for clarification on the various vehicles of expression)

But in the case of highly-advanced individuals, because their vehicles of expression have been thoroughly spiritualized during life, when they are cast-off after death, they continue to survive unimpaired and intact. And even more astounding, since these vehicles still possess a degree of internal life, they are able to "seed," or replicate, into multiple copies of themselves. By doing so, these especial vehicles become available for other fortunate individuals to mystically merge and psychically integrate into their own vehicles of expression. This of course gives a tremendous boost to the overall evolutionary advancement of humanity.

In most cases, individuals are not consciously aware that a more highly-advanced bodily-vehicle has been interwoven into their own; especially if this occurs at birth. However, if the superior vehicle is "magnetically" attracted and interwoven later in life, they may notice a sudden and profound change in their memory, emotional, intellectual or spiritual capacity; but are unable to explain what caused the sudden dramatic difference in themself.

In the case of esoteric initiates, however, they will consciously and deliberately undergo specific training in order to attract and integrate the bodily replicas of enlightened individuals so as to further their own positive development; and thereby the upward progress of humanity in general. Also worth noting is that more than one replicated vehicle can be internally integrated; and from more than one exalted source-individual.

2.1.1 The Replicated, After-Death Vehicles of Shem, Son of Noah

One noteworthy individual in the Post-Atlantean Age who replicated one of his after-death vehicles of expression is Shem, son of Noah. In Shem's case, he experienced a heightened development by having his etheric body permeated with the forces of an avatar-being. Consequently, after death Shem's specially-developed etheric body was preserved from dissolution; thereby enabling it to replicate countless copies of itself.

According to the spiritual-scientific research of Rudolf Steiner, a copy of Shem's etheric body has been interwoven in all the Hebrew descendents of Shem throughout the ages. One exalted historical figure whose mission to the Hebrews was shaped by Shem's originally-preserved etheric body that was later woven into his own was Melchizedek, the Old Testament priest-king of Salem. As Steiner stated in a lecture given on 15 February 1909, entitled "Christianity in Human Evolution, Leading Individualities and Avatar Beings":

> What was contained in the individuality of Shem was multiplied because an avatar being was incarnated in it, and all this became interwoven with all the etheric bodies of the Hebrews. In addition, Shem's own etheric body was preserved in the spiritual world so that it could be borne at a later time by Melchizedek, who was to give the Hebrews an important impulse through Abraham. (Published in *The Principle of Spiritual Economy*; 1986)

COSMIC REALMS OF EXISTENCE	INDIVIDUAL LEVELS OF EXISTENCE	VEHICLES OF EXPRESSION		SANSKRIT TERMS	DEGREES OF CONSCIOUSNESS
CELESTIAL WORLD [SPIRIT LAND]	SPIRIT	SPIRIT-BODY	THE HIGHER EGO (SELF)	ATMAN	DIVINE CONSCIOUSNESS
		LIFE-SPIRIT		BUDDHI	COSMIC CONSCIOUSNESS
		SPIRIT-SELF		MANAS	SPIRITUAL CONSCIOUSNESS
SOUL WORLD	SOUL	CONSCIOUSNESS SOUL			SOUL CONSCIOUSNESS
		INTELLECTUAL SOUL	THE LOWER EGO (SELF)	KAMA-RUPA	SELF CONSCIOUSNESS
		SENTIENT SOUL			WAKING CONSCIOUSNESS
PHYSICAL WORLD	BODY	ASTRAL BODY		LINGA-SHARIRA	DREAM CONSCIOUSNESS
		ETHERIC BODY		PRANA-JIVA	SLEEP CONSCIOUSNESS
		PHYSICAL BODY		STHULA-SHARIRA	TRANCE CONSCIOUSNESS

Figure 1: The Various Vehicles of Expression

2.1.2 The After-Death Vehicles of Zarathustra in Ancient Persia

Another important figure in ancient times whose after-death vehicles of expression were preserved and replicated was Zarathustra, the original founder of Zoroastrianism, the dualistic religion of the Ancient Persian cultural era (5067–2907 BC). In this instance, it was Zarathustra's etheric *and* astral bodies that were saved and seeded after death. Of course this is not surprising since Zarathustra is one of the twelve illustrious bodhisattvas.

Copies of Zarathustra's etheric and astral bodies were integrated into two powerful individuals who were largely responsible for the establishment of the Egypto-Chaldean cultural era (2907–707 BC) that succeeded the Ancient Persian era. The legendary Egyptian figure, Hermes, integrated a copy of Zarathustra's astral body; and the equally-legendary Hebrew figure, Moses, integrated a copy of Zarathustra's etheric body.

Since the etheric body is the "vehicle of memory," Moses had full access to the tremendous storehouse of historical recollections retained by Zarathustra. Since the astral body is the "vehicle of emotion and acquired wisdom," Hermes had access to the vast reservoir of artistic, cultural, religious, technological and natural wisdom acquired by Zarathustra.

2.2 The Redeemed, After-Death Vehicles of Christ-Jesus

Obviously, the most prized and valuable vehicles of expression in all of human history that were eminently worth preserving and replicating for posterity, and for the advancement of humanity, were those of Christ-Jesus, the saviour of the world. Through the indwelling Solar-Christos (the "Christ-Spirit") and the resultant connection with the Logos-Word, the man Jesus was able to hypostatically unite with God the Son; and to truthfully declare: "I AM the Son of God."

Through the divine power of the Son, Christ-Jesus was able to perfect and redeem his various bodily-vehicles from the negative effects of the primordial "fall" from paradise; that is, from sin, sickness, disease and death. Even though Our Saviour's exceptional vehicles were immediately preserved and exceedingly replicated after his death on the cross, they weren't immediately accessible for worthy individuals to internally integrate with their own vehicles.

It took several centuries after Christ-Jesus' death for individuals to progress enough to integrate a copy of his redeemed vehicles. Besides, in the early centuries of the Christian age, detailed historical memories of Our Saviour's life on earth were still fresh in people's minds. For a time, this was sufficient to maintain a firm, unquestioning belief in Christ-Jesus and his teachings.

2.2.1 Integrating the Redeemed Etheric Body of Christ-Jesus

Fortunately, unlike the replicated etheric bodies of Shem that were only available to his Hebrew descendents, the replicated etheric bodies of Christ-Jesus were universally available to all worthy individuals. Copies of Christ-Jesus' redeemed etheric body were the first of his vehicles to be integrated by others, since copies of his astral body and ego-imprint were much more advanced; and which therefore required further historical preparation to integrate.

Copies of Christ-Jesus' redeemed etheric body began to be integrated by several European individuals starting in the fifth century; and which continued through to the tenth century. As stated by Rudolf Steiner in a lecture given on 28 March

1909, entitled "Results of Spiritual Scientific Investigations of the Evolution of Humanity (1)":

> [H]uman beings living in the period from the fifth or sixth through the tenth centuries who had developed sufficiently received at their birth such an [etheric] imprint of the Christ-Incarnation of Jesus of Nazareth. St. Augustine [354–430] is the individual in whom such partaking in the etheric body of Christ is most clearly evident, and the great significance of his life must be attributed to this fact. (Published in *The Principle of Spiritual Economy*; 1986)

The integration of Christ-Jesus' etheric body certainly explains St. Augustine's deep theological prowess and spiritual intuition. The fact that he still possessed his own astral body and ego accounts for the immoral, hedonistic lifestyle during his adolescent years.

Another well-know historical figure who had a copy of the etheric body of Christ-Jesus woven into his own etheric body was the medieval Irish philosopher and theologian, John Scotus Erigena (c.815–c.877). Once again, this explains Erigena's deep, innate comprehension of vast philosophical history.

2.2.2 Integrating the Redeemed Astral Body of Christ-Jesus

While there were certainly many other medieval figures who were blessed with a copy of Christ-Jesus' etheric body interwoven with their own, it took until the Middle Ages—from the twelfth to the fifteenth centuries—for numerous copies of the redeemed astral body of Christ-Jesus to become available to prominent Christian figures.

When referring to the astral body in this case, it is understood to include elements of the sentient soul and the intellectual soul vehicles.[32] Since the sentient soul is the vehicle of refined feelings and emotions, those notable Christian figures of the Middle Ages who integrated a copy of Christ-Jesus' sentient-soul imprinted astral body naturally demonstrated deep emotional devotion and spiritual fervour. The most outstanding example during this time was St. Francis of Assisi (1181–1226). Another remarkable example was St. Elisabeth of Thuringia (1207–1231). Predictably, a great many Franciscan brothers and sisters also integrated a redeemed astral-body copy from Christ-Jesus during the Middle Ages.

Those fortunate individuals of the Middle Ages who integrated a copy of Christ-Jesus' intellectual-soul imprinted astral body demonstrated pronounced mental acuity and superlative reasoning capacity, rather than religious passion and fervency. The most outstanding example of this astral integration was, not surprisingly, the "philosopher-extraordinaire," St. Thomas Aquinas. Predictably as well, many other leading scholastic philosophers of the Dominican Order of Preachers possessed an integrated, intellectual-soul imprinted, astral-body copy of Christ-Jesus throughout the Middle Ages.

2.2.3 Integrating the Redeemed Ego-Imprint of Christ-Jesus

Since the consciousness soul is much more infused with the forces and impulses of the ego-self, it took more psycho-spiritual advancement for qualified individuals to historically integrate a copy of Christ-Jesus' supernal ego. It also needs to be clearly understood that the true-ego or "I-self" exclusively belongs to the individual; and therefore cannot be replicated. Nevertheless, since the activity of the spirit-ego leaves an indelible imprint of itself in the soul—particularly in the consciousness soul—by replicating the consciousness soul, a subsidiary ego-imprint *can* be copied, multiplied and shared.

Integrating a replicated ego-imprint of Christ-Jesus' consciousness-soul infused astral body only became possible during the sixteenth century. Qualified individuals during the late-Renaissance were thereby enabled to more easily unite themselves with Christ-Jesus and to self-identify as "Christo-fers"; that is, as "Christ-bearers."

Examples of exalted individuals who were advanced enough to integrate a copy of the ego-imprint of Christ-Jesus were Christian Rosenkreutz, the founder of the Rosicrucian Fraternity; Meister Eckhart (c.1260–c.1328), well-known Dominican theologian and mystic; and Johannes Tauler (c.1300–1361), German mystic and Catholic priest. As explained by Rudolf Steiner:

> The special conviction that Christ can be found in the human ego arose among those who were imbued more strongly with the copy of the consciousness soul of Jesus of Nazareth, because the ego functions in the consciousness soul. Because these individuals had within them the element of consciousness soul from the astral body of Jesus of Nazareth, the inner Christ rose resplendent within their souls, and through this astral body they came to know that the Christ within them was the Christ Himself. (From a lecture given on 25 February 1909, entitled "Christianity in Human Evolution: Leading Individualities and Avatar beings"; and published in *The Principle of Spiritual Economy*; 1909)

2.3 The After-Death Vehicles of Rudolf Steiner

Even if one doesn't accept the convincing argument that Rudolf Steiner was one of the twelve foremost bodhisattvas who serve Christ-Jesus from the etheric realm of Shambhala, the widely-held recognition that he was a highly-advanced

Christian initiate and Rosicrucian associate should certainly warrant the strong likelihood that his vehicles of expression were preserved and replicated after death. The fact that this hasn't been seriously considered and studied by dedicated anthroposophists is very unfortunate; and a further indication that his spiritual-scientific teaching has often fallen on deaf ears.

Nevertheless, this publication will begin to address this shortfall, and start to delve deeply into this important issue. As with our saviour, Christ-Jesus, *all* of Rudolf Steiner's vehicles of expression were preserved and replicated after death—his etheric body, his astral body and his ego-bearing soul vehicle. In addition, these vehicles were universally available to all qualified individuals; and not just for a select few (such as anthroposophists).

As with Christ-Jesus, there was no integration of any preserved copies of Steiner's vehicles soon after his death, because first-hand experience of his life was still vivid in the minds of many individuals who survived him. Anyone wishing to know more about Rudolf Steiner's life could converse with people who knew him personally, or who had written memoires about him.

2.3.1 Integrating a Replica of Rudolf Steiner's Etheric Body

It wasn't until the mid-1940s and 50s that replicas of Rudolf Steiner's etheric body began to be integrated in certain qualified individuals. By then, many of the individuals who personally knew Steiner had died. Nevertheless, by integrating a copy of his etheric (or "memory") body, individuals had a dim, subconscious affinity to Steiner's stored recollections. In consequence, when hearing or reading about the details of his life, this information seemed more alive and personal, akin to one's own memories. The overall result was a deep, empathetic feeling of personally understanding the details and events of Rudolf Steiner's life.

Unlike the multiple copies of Christ-Jesus' redeemed etheric body, it didn't take several centuries in order to qualify for integration; but only a couple of decades. This is quite understandable since greater preparation would be required to integrate the supernally-advanced bodily-replicas of the God-Man, Christ-Jesus.

2.3.2 Integrating a Replica of Rudolf Steiner's "Sentient" Astral Body

It wasn't until the 1960s and 70s that specific individuals were adequately prepared to integrate replicas of Rudolf Steiner's astral body. Once again, to be more specific, what were available at that time were multiple copies of Steiner's astral body that had been imprinted with the forces of the sentient soul. Since the sentient soul is the vehicle of elevated feelings, emotions, wishes and desires, those individuals who were fortunate enough to possess an interwoven astral body of Rudolf Steiner had their own astral body and soul vehicles further refined and ennobled.

Additionally, these individuals could experience something of the joys and sorrows that Rudolf Steiner had during his amazing life on earth. When reading his autobiography—*The Course of My Life*—for example, the events and struggles described were more emotionally intensified and empathetically shared; as if they were personally one's own.

An interwoven copy of Rudolf Steiner's astral body also greatly increased an emotional interest in various cultural activities—in the areas of art, education, dance, drama, religion, lifestyle, music, farming, fashion and language. This intensified cultural awareness was entirely in keeping with the "cultural revolution" that occurred during the 1960s and 70s.

Naturally for anthroposophists with an interwoven copy

of Steiner's astral body, this stimulated an increased interest in Waldorf education, eurythmy, biodynamic agriculture, the Camphill movement, esoteric Christianity, anthroposophical medicine and Mystery plays.

Unfortunately for anthroposophy, the preferential, emotional interest in the various spin-off cultural developments of spiritual science during and after the 1960s, meant that the central mission of spiritual science—the spiritualization of intellectual reasoning—was being largely ignored.

This imbalance opened the door to Luciferic influences;[33] particularly the erroneous notion that anthroposophy was a modern-day Mystery religion. It wasn't until the 1980s and 1990s that a more balanced intellectual interest in anthroposophy became a popular pursuit as well.

2.3.3 Integrating a Replica of Rudolf Steiner's "Intellectual" Astral Body

By the 1980s and 90s, sufficiently-qualified individuals were able to integrate copies of Rudolf Steiner's astral body that had been imprinted with the cognitive forces of the intellectual soul. This infused the fortunate individual with increased intellectual capacity and the ability to easily engage in complex intellectual reasoning. The foremost example of an individual with an interwoven replica of Rudolf Steiner's "intellectual" astral body was the Russian anthroposophist, Sergei O. Prokofieff (1954–2014).

In consequence, Prokofieff demonstrated prodigious intellectual energy and a herculean capacity to assimilate the writings of Rudolf Steiner. In imitation of Steiner, Prokofieff was a prolific writer, publishing at least 50 books and a number of essays. Not surprisingly, then, Prokofieff gained an enormous influence on contemporary anthroposophists.

Nevertheless, since Prokofieff retained his own ego-forces, he made some serious judgmental errors in his writing. As long as he continued to simply juxtapose and reorganize Steiner's ideas in original ways, Prokofieff's writing was faithful to Steiner's. But when he attempted to draw his own conclusions from Steiner's work, he unfortunately introduced some glaringly-mistaken ideas.[34]

Clearly the most damaging was how Prokofieff in several of his writings gave intellectual weight to the Luciferic deception that anthroposophy—instead of being a spiritual science—was a new Mystery religion founded by Rudolf Steiner. In his own words:

> The Christmas Conference is a Mystery-event. It is the beginning of the New Mysteries, the Michael Mysteries of esoteric Christianity …

> For this reason the Mystery-act of the laying of the Foundation Stone was connected for Rudolf Steiner with an enormous sacrifice—one made for the sake of the founding of the Centre of the New Mysteries, whose central point the Goetheanum was now to become.

> From all this we can see what the Goetheanum was to become … it was to be inaugurated and opened as the Mystery Centre of our time, as the very centre of a new esotericism of the West, serving Michael-Christ.

> [T]he building of the Goetheanum … this unique temple for the spiritual life …

> Thus the life path of Rudolf Steiner, who lived among us as a human being on Earth, unveils itself to us as a profound Mystery and as the archetypal image of the new path of initiation. (*Rudolf Steiner and the Founding of the New Mysteries*, 1986)

Regrettably, even though Prokofieff proudly insisted that: "I was to choose Anthroposophy as the task of my entire life, as my destiny in this world," his self-generated notion that anthroposophy was a new Mystery religion was entirely antithetical to everything that Rudolf Steiner said about spiritual science.

Equally unfortunate is the esoteric fact that many other anthroposophical thinkers who possessed an interwoven copy of Steiner's "intellectual" astral body also succumbed to the same egregious mistake as Prokofieff. This pernicious notion will be examined in more detail and thoroughly dispelled in Chapter 3.

Many non-anthroposophists also unknowingly integrated a copy of Rudolf Steiner's "intellectual" astral body during the 1980s and 90s. This naturally resulted in an expansion of philosophical activity; particularly concerning the integration of science and spirituality. One such example is *The Marriage of Sense and Soul: Integrating Science and Religion* (1999) by American philosopher, Ken Wilber (b.1949); where he argues for the possibility of a "science of spirituality." One other example is *Sacred Science: Essays on Mathematics, Physics and Spiritual Philosophy* (1995) by integral thinker, Thomas J. McFarlane (b.1964); which included such essays as: "Symmetry in Science and Religion" (1991) and " Science: Physical and Spiritual (1995).

2.4 Rudolf Steiner's Predicted Return to Earth: The First Integration of his Replicated-Ego

Most anthroposophists are aware that Rudolf Steiner predicted that he would return to earth at the end of the twentieth century or at the beginning of the twenty-first. Unfortunately, this was mistakenly understood to mean that he would physically incarnate once again. What Rudolf Steiner actually meant was that his replicated-ego would be integrated in an individual on earth for the very first time during the late-1900s or early 2000s.

As predicted, at the beginning of the twenty-first century Rudolf Steiner "returned to the earth" as an ego-imprinted astral-body replication that was integrated in a sufficiently-prepared individual for the very first time. More specifically, this ego-integration occurred in 2007 on the West Coast of North America.

Once again, it needs to be clearly understood that the true spirit-ego of every individual exclusively belongs to them alone; and therefore cannot be duplicated or shared under any circumstance. Nevertheless, since the activity of the ego leaves an indelible imprint of itself—particularly in the consciousness soul vehicle—this ego-imprint *can* be replicated and integrated into other individuals.

2.4.1 The Living Experience of an Integrated Christ-Ego

While the verbal description of a replicated-ego integration sounds dry and prosaic, the actual personal experience is anything but dull and boring. Take for example the experience of having a replicated-ego of Christ-Jesus integrated into one's own vehicles of expression. Under certain circumstances, it can actually feel as if one is actually Christ-Jesus himself. One has the experience of looking out at the world through the eyes of Christ-Jesus; and actually walking in his footsteps.

As a faithful follower of Our Saviour, it also becomes much easier to answer the question: "What would Christ-Jesus do in this particular situation?" when one possesses an integrated Christ-ego. Since moralistic impulses stem from the ego, it is also much easier to correctly determine ethical judgements of right and wrong with an integrated Christ-ego.

Possessing an integrated Christ-ego doesn't mean that one

is constantly identifying as Christ-Jesus. In a well-balanced individual, this only occurs through the conscious exercise of the will. In other words, this only takes place when the individual decides to psycho-spiritually merge with their integrated Christ-ego.

Tragically, there have been rare instances where an individual hasn't been entirely prepared for, or who doesn't completely understand, the phenomenon of possessing an integrated Christ-ego. In these cases, the unfortunate individual succumbs to the messianic delusion that they are actually Christ-Jesus. This of course has resulted in mental and emotional imbalance, until the delusional notion is corrected.

2.4.2 The Living Experience of an Integrated Ego-Replica of Rudolf Steiner

For the individual possessing an integrated ego-replica of Rudolf Steiner, it is also a unique and exhilarating experience. In this case, one looks out at the world through the eyes of Rudolf Steiner; and literally walks in his footsteps. When attending a contemporary anthroposophical event, or reading a newly-published anthroposophical book, one experiences them as Rudolf Steiner would experience them. Even everyday activities such as driving a car or watching a movie, are experienced as Rudolf Steiner would experience them.

And once again, since moral judgements are formed by the ego, the integrated ego-replica of Rudolf Steiner is capable of passing moral judgement on what is currently taking place within anthroposophy. One experiences the right and wrong of contemporary anthroposophical activities, events and initiatives (or lack of them) as Rudolf Steiner would experience them.

Since there are multiple copies of Rudolf Steiner's ego-imprinted astral body waiting to be integrated, his "return to earth" is not just a single event; but the beginning of a new phase in the development of anthroposophy. Imagine the combined effect of a large number of individuals in which the replicated-ego of Rudolf Steiner is active. Just think how this has the potential to positively transform anthroposophy, to correct the internal errors that have surreptitiously crept in, and to heal the karmic divisions that have stunted positive development over the years. These are the crucial issues that will be addressed in the next Chapter.

CHAPTER 3

THE 21ST CENTURY RENEWAL OF ANTHROPOSOPHY

3.1 Resolving the Karmic Conflict Between Platonists and Aristotelians

AS WELL AS predicting his "return to earth" (that is, the first integration of his replicated-ego) at the beginning of the twenty-first century, Rudolf Steiner also indicated that many anthroposophists born in the nineteenth century would hastily re-incarnate by the end of the twentieth century; as stated in the following:

> For over the Anthroposophical Society a destiny hovers: many of those in the Anthroposophical Society to-day [1924] will have to come again to the Earth before, and at the end of, the twentieth century (from a lecture given on 18 July 1924; and published in *Karmic Relationships: Esoteric Studies Vol. VI*)

The reason for this unusually-brief after-death interval was to enable a profound karmic interchange between the

45

historical Christian followers of Plato, and the historical Christian followers of Aristotle. Unless one has seriously studied the spiritual struggle of Christianity over the past two thousand years, it is highly unlikely that one has any knowledge or understanding of the profound effect that ancient Greek philosophy has had on Christian development.

3.1.1 The Fundamental Dichotomy Between Platonists and Aristotelians

Even though Aristotle was a pupil in Plato's Academy for about twenty years, there were still some fundamental differences between their respective philosophies. Throughout the succeeding centuries, on the basis of these ideological differences, the followers of Plato and the followers of Aristotle became increasingly more antagonistic toward each other. Unfortunately, this philosophical conflict had serious societal repercussions throughout the Christian Age.

The fundamental dichotomy between Platonism and Aristotelianism is based on a fundamental duality of Nature—the existence of a physical world, and the existence of a spiritual world. Simply stated, Platonic philosophy placed singular importance on the spiritual world; while largely disregarding the physical world as an inferior creation of the spiritual world. Aristotelian philosophy, on the other hand, place equal importance on the physical world and the spiritual world; regarding the physical-sensory world as a faithful reflection of the spiritual world.

Consequently, Platonists didn't view the changeable, transient physical world as worthy of intellectual study; only the eternal, unchanging ideas ("archetypes") of the spiritual world. The Aristotelians, however, viewed the physical world as eminently worthy of intellectual and sensory study because it was a faithful reflection of the spiritual world.

Consequently, a great deal of spiritual knowledge can be intellectually acquired by studying the physical world.

3.1.2 The Influence and Opposition of Platonism and Aristotelianism during the Christian Age

In the early centuries of Christianity, many renowned Church Fathers (the "Patristic philosophers") endeavoured to use Platonism in an effort to lend strong philosophical support to the nascent Christian theology that was constantly coming under ideological attack. One of the foremost Church Fathers who combined Platonic philosophy with Christian theology was St. Augustine of Hippo (354–430). As he explained in his *Confessions* (Book VIII):

> Simplicianus congratulated me that I had not fallen upon the writings of other philosophers, which were full of fallacies and deceit, "after the beggarly elements of this world (Col 2:8)," whereas in the Platonists, at every turn, the pathway led to belief in God and his Word.

The "Platonic-Christianity" of St. Augustine was widely accepted throughout medieval Europe and reached its culmination during the High Middle Ages in the School of Chartres. The celebrated French school was the centre of twelfth-century Platonism in the West; and boasted such illustrious scholars as Bernard of Chartres (d. c.1124), Thierry of Chartres (d. c.1150), William of Conches (c.1090–c.1154), Alain de Lille (1128–1202) and John of Salisbury (c.1110–1180). Instruction in the school was presented pictorially, rather than intellectually.[35]

In the thirteenth and fourteenth centuries, with the rise of scholasticism,[36] interest in Platonic philosophy was supplanted by an explosion of interest in the philosophy of Aristotle. As previously mentioned in Chapter 1, the preeminent philosopher who brilliantly reconciled Aristotelian philosophy with Christian theology was St.

Thomas Aquinas. By convincingly arguing the Aristotelian concept that the physical-sensory world was worthy of study—from which knowledge of the spiritual world and of God can be deduced—St. Thomas opened the door to the scientific study of universal creation.

The "Aristotelian-Christianity" of St. Thomas was hugely influential throughout Western society—and was strongly defended by the Dominican Order—even into the twentieth century. Nevertheless, St. Thomas' Aristotelian influence has also been continuously resisted by Platonic-minded Augustinians and Franciscans within the Catholic Church, who tend to de-emphasize scientific intellectual reasoning in favour of mystical experience and feelings.

From the very beginning in ancient Greece, Platonic critics vehemently blamed Aristotle for directing intellectual attention away from the spiritual world down to the physical world. All the problems connected with materialistic, secular society were blamed on Aristotle. Conversely, Aristotelian critics angrily accused Plato of falsely denigrating the physical-sensory world—an important aspect of God's creation. By doing so, Platonists were seen to have their "heads in the clouds," ignoring the vital lessons of the physical world.[37]

3.1.3 Reconciling Platonists and Aristotelians through Anthroposophy

Esoterically speaking, the animosity between the Platonist-Christians and the Aristotelian-Christians was so pronounced that over the centuries they would actually avoid incarnating on earth at the same time. At a certain point, this needless and continuing karmic conflict was beginning to seriously impede and impair the future development of Christianity.

In order to reconcile these two powerful philosophical streams of Christianity, St. Michael the archangel convened a mighty supersensible conclave of Platonists and Aristotelians during the first half of the nineteenth century. St. Michael presented the illustrious gathering with a divinely-sanctioned strategy to heal the division between the two philosophies; thereby enabling the progressive advancement of Christianity into the future. A major component of this cosmic strategy was the establishment of anthroposophy in order to lead intellectual reasoning back to the spiritual world.[38]

To accomplish this task, Aristotle himself (Rudolf Steiner) would lead a group of Aristotelians into physical incarnation during the second half of the nineteenth century. Once anthroposophy had been successfully established at the beginning of the twentieth century, then the Platonists would incarnate during the second half of the twentieth century.

The deceased Aristotelians who had assisted Rudolf Steiner in establishing anthroposophy would then expeditiously re-incarnate so that they would be together on earth with the Platonists at the beginning of the twenty-first century. Through the supersensible knowledge of anthroposophy, the modern-day Platonists would come to realize the crucial importance of developing intellectual reasoning, such that it can effectively access the spiritual world.

Furthermore, by learning through anthroposophy that mankind was destined for a time to exclusively focus on the physical, material world in order to master it—and to develop freedom and ego-independence—the Platonists would no longer disparage the work of Aristotle, but willingly choose to unite with him.

3.1.4 The Need for Anthroposophical Platonists to Develop and Spiritualize Intellectual Reasoning

In order to successfully renew anthroposophy in the twenty-first century, it is necessary that those members who are intuitively disposed to Platonism should begin to recognize and acknowledge their Platonic disposition. This is necessary because, for many anthroposophists, their Platonic disposition from previous lives operates entirely at a subconscious level; and has consequently hindered the full development of spiritual science.

This hidden karmic affinity to Platonism will very often determine certain predictable personality traits. One such prominent personality trait is a lack of interest in rigorous intellectual reasoning; which results in a disinterest in studying mathematics, philosophy and science. A second, related personality trait is a preferential affinity for subjects that arouse emotions, feelings, desires and passions; which results in a preferential interest in the fine arts, religion, drama, dance and music.

As a foreseen but unfortunate result, a great many Platonic anthroposophists focus their time and energy on the secondary, cultural spin-offs of anthroposophy (such as eurythmy, mystery dramas, biodynamic farming, Christian Community religion, Waldorf education or Camphill activity); to the neglect of prioritizing the spiritualization of their intellectual reasoning—which is the principle mission of anthroposophical *spiritual science*.

3.2 Acknowledging Anthroposophy as Spiritual Science and not as Mystery-Religion

The subconscious tendency of Platonic anthroposophists to minimize, de-emphasize and even evade anthroposophy's fundamental purpose as a *science* of the spirit has resulted in a pernicious notion that has seriously impeded anthroposophy's spiritual mission. The erroneous idea that anthroposophy is some sort of modern-day Mystery-religion, or revival of the ancient pagan Mysteries is entirely contrary to everything Rudolf Steiner has said about anthroposophy.

Steiner was consistently clear that the various pagan Mystery Centres of antiquity once functioned as powerful and influential institutions of esoteric knowledge (or "gnosis"). This secretly-guarded wisdom inspired the major cultural developments of the past; such as the arts, music, drama, education, religion and politics. Over time, as prehistoric humanity gradually lost its innate, dream-like clairvoyance, perception of the spiritual world grew darker and darker. The black shadow of spiritual nightfall also fell on the ancient Mysteries.

The destined demise of these pagan Mysteries, and the resultant inability for human individuals to perceptually access the spiritual world, necessitated the incarnation of the God-Man, Christ-Jesus, in order to regain entry into the heavenly realms. Furthermore, Christ-Jesus superseded the obsolete pagan Mysteries with the new "Christ Mysteries"—the "Mysteries of the Son." As Steiner definitively declared in a lecture given on 27 November 1906, entitled, "Esoteric Christianity: The Gospel of St. John and Ancient Mysteries":

> At the time of Christ Jesus, to the Mysteries of the Spirit were added the Mysteries of the Son, and these have been ever since the time of Christ. The Mysteries of the Father—the Mysteries of the Future—are only cultivated in a very small circle. The Mysteries of the Son are cultivated in the Rosicrucian Mystery which is also Christian, for those who require a Christianity that is armed to meet all Wisdom ... Today we will concern ourselves with the Mysteries of the Son, and see how they differ from the ancient heathen Mysteries. If we would grasp what a mighty step forward has been taken by the coming of Christianity ...

3.2.1 Anthroposophy Does Not Re-Establish the Gnosis of the Ancient Mysteries

The esoteric knowledge and wisdom that was secretly acquired and jealously guarded within the confines of the ancient Mysteries—the "gnosis"—was specifically suited to prehistoric times when humanity was unfolding and developing the sentient soul. Characteristically, then, this gnostic wisdom was vividly pictorial rather than sharply conceptual; and dreamily clairvoyant rather than supersensibly awake. Predictably, as humanity began to develop the powers of the intellectual soul during the Graeco-Roman cultural era, the harsh light of scientific reason and logic gradually supplanted the ancient gnosis.

This ancient mystery-wisdom became even more anachronistic when humanity began to unfold the consciousness soul starting in the fifteenth century. When Rudolf Steiner founded anthroposophy in the twentieth century as a spiritual science, it was in conformity with the requirements of consciousness soul development. In modern times, verifiable spiritual knowledge had to be obtained in full conscious awareness, communicated in clear intellectual concepts, and authenticated with strict, science-like reasoning. True spiritual knowledge can no longer be acquired like the gnosis of the ancient Mysteries; that is, in dream-like, figurative imagery obtained in a deep-trance, out-of-body condition.

So, for anthroposophists to seriously entertain the entirely regressive notion that the mission of spiritual science is to renew the ancient Mystery-gnosis completely ignores everything that Rudolf Steiner has repeatedly declared. In one of his *Anthroposophical Leading Thoughts* (1973), entitled "Gnosis and Anthroposophy," he succinctly stated:

> Anthroposophy strives for this new understanding, which … cannot be a renewal of the Gnosis. For the content of the Gnosis was the way of knowledge of the Sentient Soul, while Anthroposophy—in a completely new way—must draw forth a content no less rich from the

Spiritual [Consciousness] Soul.

Anthroposophy cannot be a revival of the Gnosis. For the latter depended on the development of the Sentient Soul; while Anthroposophy must evolve out of the Spiritual Soul, in the light of [St.] Michael's activity, a new understanding of Christ and of the World. Gnosis was the way of Knowledge preserved from ancient time ...

3.2.2 Anthroposophy's Mission is not to Renew the Ancient Mysteries

It's rather astounding to think that as recently as April 2016, the North American Collegium of the School of Spiritual Science issued a report to members which stated:

Rudolf Steiner's characterization of the re-founding of the Anthroposophical Society and the founding of the School for [sic] Spiritual Science as a renewal of the ancient Mysteries and a founding of the New Mysteries.

This theme of the renewal of the Mysteries will be taken up for a number of years, and we are inviting you as a member of the School, individually or with others, to take up this theme in your own way.

Aside from the fact that such statements indicate a disturbing lack of understanding regarding anthroposophical spiritual science, it also demonstrates an equally disturbing ignorance of the ancient Mysteries. For example, how exactly are these ancient Mysteries to be renewed; considering that such a venture is either hopelessly futile, impossible to accomplish or entirely undesirable to attempt?

For instance, the ancient Mysteries were immense and complex institutions situated in difficult locations with elaborate marble buildings and huge sacred temples surrounded by elegant statuary. As centres of esoteric learning, the Mysteries involved an elaborate system of mystic instructors, initiate students, courses of study, religious rituals and public festivals. To renew such an institution today would involve millions (perhaps billions) of dollars—so obviously this won't be an anthroposophical undertaking anytime soon.

The ancient Mysteries were also highly secretive institutions that jealously guarded their gnostic knowledge under pain of death. Obviously as anthroposophists such a restrictive policy would be quite undesirable to renew; since the statutes of the Anthroposophical Society state:

> The Anthroposophical Society is in no sense a secret society, but is entirely public. (Statute 4)

> All publications [ie: knowledge] of the Society shall be public, in the same sense as are those of other public societies. The publications of the School of Spiritual Science will form no exception as regards this public character; (Statute 8)

The leadership positions and the initiate students in the ancient Mysteries were exclusively restricted to men; women were absolutely forbidden to participate. In this day and age of gender equality, obviously modern-day anthroposophists will not be too anxious about renewing this particular discriminatory policy of the Mysteries.

The ancient Mysteries were religious institutions; in fact one of their designations, other than "Mystery-Schools" and "Mystery-Centres," was "Mystery-Religions." As such, these institutions incorporated religious ritual (such as animal sacrifice and cultic initiations); and diligently practiced the worship of specific pagan gods and goddesses (such as Demeter, Persephone, Dionysus, Apollo, Isis, Serapis and Mithras). Rudolf Steiner repeatedly emphasized that anthroposophy is a spiritual *science*, and is in no way a *religion*:

> This spiritual science is not trying to found either a new

religion or a new religious sect of any kind.

Spiritual science does not want to usurp the place of Christianity; on the contrary it would like to be the instrument in making Christianity understood. (From a lecture given on 13 July 1914 and published in *Anthroposophy and Christianity*; 1985).

Therefore, this integral religious aspect of the ancient Mysteries can't possibly be renewed in the context of anthroposophical spiritual science.

A further component of the ancient Mysteries that would be impossible—as well as entirely undesirable—to renew was the dangerous method that was used to directly experience the spiritual world in order to obtain sacred knowledge (gnosis). In this case, initiates were hypnotically placed in a catatonic, death-like trance for three days; which was referred to as the "temple sleep." During this time, the initiate's soul vehicle was temporarily separated from the physical body; thereby allowing the initiate to sojourn in the spiritual world.

However, in order for the initiate to recall their out-of-body experience, part of the etheric (or memory) body had to be separated as well. Since the etheric body is also known as the "life body," this partial separation placed the initiate perilously close to death for three days. Consequently, the comatose physical body needed to be carefully guarded during the temple sleep. Unfortunately, on occasion the trance-initiate was not successfully revived. For obvious reasons, then, this dangerous and obsolete ancient Mystery practice is not likely to be renewed by today's anthroposophists.

Lastly, the ancient Mysteries were pagan religious institutions that were superseded in the course of human development by Christianity. Furthermore, much of the gnostic-wisdom of the Mysteries was cautiously elicited from Luciferic spirits. As explained by Rudolf Steiner in a lecture given on 15 November 1919:

> [G]oing back to the primeval origins of human existence, we find that the sources of pagan wisdom always lie with luciferic beings.
>
> In olden times the wisdom needed for the progress of humanity could be obtained only from a luciferic source; hence the initiates were obliged to receive it from that source and at the same time to take upon themselves the obligation not to yield to the aspirations of the luciferic beings.
>
> Lucifer's intention was to convey the wisdom to humanity in such a way that it would induce people to abandon the path of earth evolution and take a path leading to a super-earthly sphere, a sphere aloof from the earth. The luciferic beings inculcated their wisdom into human beings but their desire was that it would make them turn away from the earth, without passing through earthly evolution. Lucifer wants to abandon the earth to its fate, to win humankind for a kingdom alien to the kingdom of Christ. (Published in *The Influences of Lucifer and Ahriman*; 1993)

Since anthroposophy is a Christ-centred spiritual science, it would be entirely regressive and counter-evolutionary to make any attempt to renew the ancient, Luciferically-inspired pagan Mysteries.

3.2.3 The Christmas Conference did not Transform Anthroposophy into the "New Mysteries"

Not long after an important nine-day anthroposophical gathering (from 24 December 1923 to 01 January 1924)—known as the "Christmas Conference")—a perniciously-false notion of anthroposophy began to be promulgated by some influential anthroposophists.[39] The deleterious notion was that Rudolf Steiner organized the Christmas Conference in order to establish the "New Mysteries." In other words, everything that Steiner had previously emphasized about anthroposophy being a spiritual science was entirely negated at the Conference; and instead, he decided to suddenly transform it into a modern-day Mystery-religion.

Such an idea is blatantly preposterous on strictly rational grounds. Logically speaking, why would Rudolf Steiner—from the very beginning—establish a spiritual science in conformity with the requirements of consciousness soul development; and then regress back to becoming a Mystery religion (which only had relevance during sentient-soul development in ancient times.)

Furthermore, the idea of Rudolf Steiner founding some sort of Mystery-religion is nowhere indicated in any of the written records of the Christmas Conference. It's abundantly clear from the Conference records that Rudolf Steiner's primary intent was to join the anthroposophical movement, the Anthroposophical Society and the newly formed School of Spiritual Science into one overarching organization—the General Anthroposophical Society—with himself as its first president.

This was a momentous achievement that is little understood and appreciated by most anthroposophists, even today. Unlike the super-secretive Mystery-centres of ancient times, and the hidden esoteric brotherhoods of the Christian age, the General Anthroposophical Society is an entirely open and public society with a Western esoteric content—the first such esoteric organization in human history.[40] As stated by Rudolf Steiner in the Opening Lecture at the Conference on 24 December 1923:

[T]he Anthroposophical Society must stand before the world just like any other society that may be founded for, let us say, scientific or similar purposes. It must differ from all these other societies solely on account of the [esoteric] content that flows through its veins. The form in which people come together in it can, in future, no longer be different from that of any other society.

Herewith I have at least hinted at the fundamental conditions which must be placed before our hearts at the beginning of *our Conference for the founding of the General Anthroposophical Society* [emphasis added].

As succinctly indicated in the quotation above, there is absolutely no mention in the Conference records of founding some undefined "New Mysteries."

As an integral part of the General Anthroposophical Society, Rudolf Steiner also established a "School of Spiritual Science" at the Christmas Conference—*not* a "School of Mystery-Gnosis." Unlike the ancient secretive Mystery Schools, the School of Spiritual Science established by Steiner was open, transparent and publically accessible. He intended the School to be modeled after a three-year university program; but with a spiritual-scientific content. As explained by Steiner at the Conference on 25 December 1923:

The Anthroposophical Society sees the School of Spiritual Science in Dornach as the centre for its activity. The School will be composed of three classes after the manner of other universities. (Statute 5)

The purpose of the Anthroposophical Society will be the furtherance of spiritual research; that of the School of Spiritual Science will be this research itself. (Statute 9)

Regarding the Second Goetheanum (whose construction began in 1924 and completed in 1928), this was never described as a "Temple of the New Mysteries" in the Conference records. Instead, it was regarded as the *headquarters* of the General Anthroposophical Society and the *university* of the School of Spiritual Science; as indicated in the following Statute statements:

> The headquarters of the Anthroposophical Society is at the Goetheanum. (Statute 11)

> [T]he existence of an institution such as the Goetheanum in Dornach, in its capacity as a School of Spiritual Science. (Stature 4)

3.2.4 The New Christ-Mysteries are far Superior to the Ancient Pagan Mysteries

Rudolf Steiner was very clear that Christ-Jesus himself established the "new Christ-Mysteries," also known as the "Mysteries of the Son," to supplant and supersede the obsolete pagan Mysteries of the past. Furthermore, these new Christ-Mysteries were far superior to any of the ancient Mysteries. In his own words:

> [E]soteric [Mystery] Christianity is essentially deeper than all oriental esoteric [Mysteries]. The truth is, the Christian [Mystery] esotericism is the most profound which has ever been brought to mankind.
> Christian [Mystery] esotericism was brought to the earth by that very Being Himself with whom one must be united. It is a question of belief in the *divinity* of Christ.

> At the time of Christ Jesus, to the Mysteries of the Spirit were added the Mysteries of the Son, and these have been ever since the time of Christ. The Mysteries of the Father—the Mysteries of the Future—are only cultivated in a very small circle. The Mysteries of the Son are cultivated in the Rosicrucian Mystery which is also Christian, for those who require a Christianity that is armed to meet all Wisdom.

> Today we will concern ourselves with the Mysteries of the

Son, and see how they differ from the ancient heathen Mysteries. If we would grasp what a mighty step forward has been taken by the coming of Christianity. (From a lecture given 27 November 1906, entitled "Esoteric Christianity: The Gospel of St. John and Ancient Mysteries")

As a spiritual science, anthroposophy's declared mission is to study, examine and intellectually comprehend the new Christ-Mysteries. It makes absolutely no sense for anthroposophists to think that Rudolf Steiner would arrogantly displace the sublime Son-Mysteries of Christ-Jesus with his own New-Mysteries. Such an idea is inconceivably preposterous.

Likewise, referring to these New-Mysteries as "Michael-Mysteries" is equally outrageous. What Christ-centred anthroposophist would seriously entertain the notion that St. Michael, the great and loyal emissary of Christ-Jesus, would substitute his own Michael-Mysteries for the transcendent Mysteries of the Son? Besides, as the sponsor and inspirer of anthroposophy, St. Michael's mission is to intellectually comprehend the Christ-Mysteries in an intellectual, spiritual-scientific way; not to regressively establish some alternate Michael-Mysteries of his own.

In order to effectively renew anthroposophy in the twenty-first century, it's important for anthroposophists to realized how profoundly different the new Christ-Mysteries are from the ancient pagan-Mysteries. For instance, the new Christ-Mysteries do not refer to a school, a temple or an institution; they refer to a person—a divine Person, the Son—hypostatically united in Christ-Jesus.

Everything about the divine nature of the Trinitarian God is infinitely beyond the capacity of the human mind to totally comprehend. In Christian terminology, then, every detail of God's nature is a "mystery." In the case of Christ-Jesus, since his human nature was, and continues to be, hypostatically united with God the Son, all aspects of his life on earth have been eternally divinized; and are therefore sacred "mysteries."

As such, his birth is a mystery; his childhood is a mystery; his baptism is a mystery; his teachings are a mystery; his miracles are a mystery; his transfiguration is a mystery; his crucifixion is a mystery; his resurrection is a mystery; and his ascension is a mystery. The Catholic devotion of the Rosary identifies twenty such mysteries in the life of Christ-Jesus.[41]

Whereas the ancient Mystery-religions secretly acquired, preserved and taught mystery-truth; in regard to the Mysteries of the Son, Christ-Jesus *is* the mystery-truth that he proclaims. Hence his definitive, biblical declaration: "I AM the Truth" (John 14:6). Furthermore, unlike the ancient Mystery-religions, the new Christ-mysteries are not safeguarded within an architectural Mystery-temple building; but instead abide within the living "temple" of the human heart.

3.2.5 Misunderstood Statements by Rudolf Steiner about the School of Spiritual Science

Unfortunately, but not surprisingly, certain brief statements made by Rudolf Steiner about the School of Spiritual Science have been entirely misconstrued in order to advance the faulty notion that anthroposophy is a "renewal of the ancient Mysteries."

As previously indicated, the records of the actual Christmas Conference made no mention of the ancient Mysteries in any connection with anthroposophy during the entire proceedings. However, in a lecture given shortly after the Conference on 22 April 1924 entitled, "The Mysteries of Ephesus. The Aristotelian Categories," Steiner stated the following:

It is indeed the case that when that spiritual impulse which has gone forth from here, from the Goetheanum through the Christmas Foundation meeting, really finds its way into the life of the Anthroposophical Society—(the Society leading on to the [School of Spiritual Science] Classes partially begun)—this Anthroposophical Society will provide the foundation for the Mysteries of the future. The future life of the Mysteries must consciously and deliberately be planted by this Anthroposophical Society.

Providing "the foundation for the Mysteries of the future" does not mean that Rudolf Steiner *founded* some undefined "New Mysteries" at the Christmas Conference. The Mysteries of the future are esoterically known as the "Mysteries of the Father." This divine wisdom will at some time in the future supersede the Mysteries of the Son, which are currently being studied in the Rosicrucian schools (including the School of Spiritual Science). As previously quoted from Rudolf Steiner:

> The Mysteries of the Father—the Mysteries of the Future—are only cultivated in a very small circle. The Mysteries of the Son are cultivated in the Rosicrucian Mystery which is also Christian … (From a lecture given 27 November 1906, entitled "Esoteric Christianity: The Gospel of St. John and Ancient Mysteries")

What Steiner was clearly indicating with his misinterpreted statement was that the Rosicrucian-sponsored School of Spiritual Science, as well as currently studying the new Christ-Mysteries, must also begin to prepare the esoteric foundation for the spiritual-scientific study of the Father-Mysteries in the future.

Further statements that Rudolf Steiner made after the Christmas Conference in connection with the School of Spiritual Science are even more easily misinterpreted without placing them in the broader context of many other clarifying statements that he made. Take for example the following statement from Class Lesson 6 which was given on 21 March

1924:

> [T]his School must be regarded as being established by the spiritual world itself.
>
> This is the essence of all Mystery Schools, that people appointed by the spiritual powers of the world speak in them. The essence of the Mystery Schools must so remain. (Published in *The First Class Lessons and Mantras: The Michael School Meditative Path in Nineteen Steps*; 2017)

Once again, what is expressed here is not the faulty notion that anthroposophy or the School of Spiritual Science is a renewal of the ancient pagan Mysteries. What Rudolf Steiner is explicitly saying is that the ancient Mysteries were initiatives of the spiritual world; and that in this particular respect, the School of Spiritual Science is also an initiative of the spiritual world. As such, both are esoteric institutions.

However, in other respects the School of Spiritual Science bears no similarity with the ancient Mysteries. For example: it's not super-secretive; it's not restricted to men; it's not a religion; it doesn't involve trance-initiation; it doesn't have an exclusive gnosis; it's not pre-Christian (pagan); and it doesn't include dangerous physical ordeals.

One further instance of comments made by Rudolf Steiner soon after the Christmas Conference that are incredibly easy to misconstrue if taken superficially was given on 02 May 1924 in a presentation of Class Lesson 8:

> Here in the School for Spiritual Science everything that lived in the Mysteries, at the time when the Mysteries were truly flourishing, should really come to life again in the proper form for our time and for future times. The golden age of the Mysteries was already past when the greatest, yet most veiled of all mysteries—the Mystery of Golgotha—took place in world history ... it was followed by a period in human history and evolution when the

Mysteries receded ... But now the time has come when the mysteries must come to life again in a form that is right for us today in the fullest sense of the word ... For then it will be recognized that the Goetheanum had the task of renewing the life of the Mysteries. My dear brothers and sisters, only if we are permeated with the will to regard the School in this manner—as representing a renewal of the Mysteries in the fullest sense—only then do we stand in the right relationship to these Mysteries and also to this School.

The key to correctly understanding this quotation is in knowing precisely what Rudolf Steiner meant by "the Mysteries ... should really come to life again in the proper form for our time." The "proper form" that Steiner has repeatedly declared is the esoteric form of a "spiritual science"—that is, the ancient, pictorial Mystery-gnosis has to be entirely transformed into modern-day, intellectually-understood, spiritual-scientific knowledge.[42] Moreover, this is the proper form of esoteric knowledge that is to be fully alive and devoutly studied within the School of Spiritual Science. As well, since there is so much misunderstanding regarding the word "Mystery," the School of Spiritual Science is best described as a modern-day *esoteric* school, rather than a completely-transformed *Mystery* school.[43]

3.2.6 Acknowledging and Rejecting the Seductive Luciferic Intrusion into Anthroposophy

At first it might seem rather bewildering that so many prominent and regular anthroposophists continue to illogically accept the preposterous notion that spiritual science is (or should be) some sort of "renewed Mystery-religion." But once it is clearly understood that founding a pagan Mystery-religion during the developmental period of the consciousness soul is entirely anachronistic, retrogressive and degenerative, then it becomes abundantly clear from whence comes this pervasively-seductive impulse.

Few anthroposophists sufficiently recognize and understand that anthroposophy—as a crucially-important evolutionary-initiative of the spiritual world, is under constant assailment from the opposing spirits of darkness. As with Christ's body the Church, their futile and evil intention is to destroy any positive spiritual influence in the world.

These assaults may be external, and come in the form of government restrictions (by the Nazis, for example); or terrorist attacks (the arson of the first Goetheanum, for example); or hostile media-criticism (by renegade Jesuits, for example). Destructive impulses may also be subtly internal, and therefore more difficult to detect. Such is the pernicious notion that anthroposophy is a modern-day Mystery-religion.

Anthroposophists recognize that one of the foremost spirits of darkness is Lucifer; and that one of his defining characteristics is an insatiable desire to regressively return to the past, to deleteriously "turn back the clock of time." This is because Lucifer nostalgically longs to regain his previous heavenly-estate that he enjoyed before his ignominious "fall from grace."[44]

Knowing this, it's easy to conclude that the regressive impulse to transform modern-day spiritual science into a Mystery-religion from the past is Luciferically inspired. By diverting anthroposophical attention away from its true mission as a spiritual science, Lucifer can surreptitiously undermine and insidiously corrupt anthroposophy from within.

In order to positively renew anthroposophy in the twenty-first century it is absolutely necessary to acknowledge and thoroughly reject the Luciferic notion that spiritual science is instead a modern-day Mystery-religion. As a spiritual science, anthroposophy can certainly study the Mystery-religions of the past. This, however, doesn't automatically transform anthroposophy into a Mystery-religion; any more than the science of anthropology suddenly transforms into a tribal-cult when it studies the primitive cultures of the past. Similarly, performing Mystery-plays at the Goetheanum doesn't transform it into a Mystery-temple; any more than performing a Christmas nativity-play at elementary school transforms it into a Christian church.

Clearly, one of the main reasons that the Luciferic-notion of "spiritual science being a Mystery-religion" gained such a pervasive foothold amongst anthroposophists was that Rudolf Steiner himself was not alive on earth to immediately dispel the ridiculous notion. However, with the increasing integration of the ego-replica of Rudolf Steiner in the twenty-first century, more and more anthroposophists will reject any Luciferic intrusion into spiritual science because they experientially will know that this is exactly what Rudolf Steiner would do today.

3.3 Advancing the Unfinished Work of Rudolf Steiner

Admittedly, for any dedicated esotericist or sincere clairvoyant, Rudolf Steiner is a very "tough act to follow." No one in recorded history has publically demonstrated a more profound supersensible ability to access and transcribe the Akashic Records. Likewise, no one has demonstrated greater clairvoyant knowledge of the celestial hierarchy, human physiology, post-mortem existence, karmic relationships, Rosicrucian theosophy, the mystery of Christ-Jesus, ancient Mystery-wisdom, elemental beings, the kingdoms of nature, or esoteric history.

So, when Rudolf Steiner leaves some anthroposophical initiative unfinished because of his premature death, is it possible for others to continue his work? A somewhat similar question could be posed regarding Christ-Jesus. Since no human being is equal to the divine nature of Christ-Jesus, due to his own premature death on the cross, is it at all possible for lesser persons to continue his salvational mission on earth?

In both instances, not only is it possible to continue the spiritual work of Rudolf Steiner and of Christ-Jesus; but it is critically necessary to do so for positive human development, and morally expected to do so as the right course of action. Also applicable in both instances, the followers of Rudolf Steiner and Christ-Jesus are certainly not expected to surpass the supernal achievements of these extraordinary way-showers; but rather to follow in their footsteps and contribute in whatever small capacity they are able to do.

Countless Christian saints and followers have positively contributed to the historical development of Christianity, despite the fact that they were nowhere near the developmental level of Christ-Jesus. So too with anthroposophy; a great many followers have positively contributed to its growth and development over the years, despite being sorely unequal to Rudolf Steiner in spiritual development.

The fact that in both instances followers are expected to positively contribute what they can is one of the primary reasons that Rudolf Steiner and Christ-Jesus chose to remain in the superphysical realm for an extended period of time after death. If they continually appeared on earth, most followers would not be encouraged to take action themselves; but instead would overly rely on Steiner or Christ-Jesus to accomplish everything. This would negatively affect the individual exercise of free-will; and thereby stunt the necessary personal development of the followers.

3.3.1 Further Developing the Classes of the School of Spiritual Science

One of the most familiar initiatives of Rudolf Steiner that continues to remain incomplete up to the present day is the School of Spiritual Science—more specifically—the three Classes. When Steiner established the School of Spiritual Science at the Christmas Concert, he originally envisioned it functioning like a typical university with a graded, sequential program of three Classes. The content or subject matter of these three Classes would naturally be deeply esoteric; and students would progress from the First Class to the Second Class to the Third Class.

Unfortunately, due to his premature death in 1925, Rudolf Steiner was only able to formulate nineteen lessons for the First Class. Two other sections of the First Class remain incomplete;[45] as well as the entire Second and the Third Classes.

Most members of the School of Spiritual Science appear content to repeat the nineteen lessons of the First Class over and over again, without any visible desire to move on to a Second Class. But this is like being endlessly stuck in first-year university with no hope of ever graduating. Will there never be a Second or a Third Class unless Rudolf Steiner himself re-incarnates on earth to complete them?

Obviously, like any progressive reformer who has successfully established a worthwhile venture or initiative on earth, Rudolf Steiner would expect future generations of his followers to contribute what they can to continue, refresh and advance what was left behind. Otherwise, the forward momentum stagnates, rigidifies and eventually dies out. So too with the classes of the School of Spiritual Science.

In order to contribute something positive to the incomplete classes of the School of Spiritual Science, it's logically necessary to determine Steiner's vision for these Classes: "What are the Classes meant to accomplish; what is the goal?" It's only by reasonably answering this question that one can begin to contemplate how best to realize Steiner's vision.

Rudolf Steiner himself, in the newsletter, *To The Members* (20 January 1924), gave some indication of what the three Classes in the School of Spiritual Science were intended to do:

> There will be people, however, who would wish to have a part in the spiritual world presented in ideas, to rise from ideas to forms of expression taken from the spiritual world itself. And there will be others who would want to get to know the roads to the world of the spirit so that they might follow them in their own souls.
>
> For such people there will be the three Classes of the School. Work done in them will lead to ever higher levels of esotericism. The School will guide the individual concerned to regions of the spiritual world which cannot be revealed in form of ideas. For these it will be necessary to find means of giving expression to Imaginations, Inspirations and Intuitions.

While this description is certainly brief, it nevertheless conveys a great deal of pertinent information regarding the three Classes. For one, the three Classes are specifically designed for anthroposophists who wish to have a deeper esoteric understanding of the spiritual world. Moreover, this deeper understanding of the spiritual world is not conveyed primarily through intellectual concepts, but through direct supersensible perceptions. In other words, individual supersensible forms of the spiritual world (Imaginations) are described, as well as their meaningful spiritual inter-relationships (Inspirations), together with communications from the various celestial beings (Intuitions).

As a result, the nineteen lessons of the First Class are vibrantly visual, pictorial, artistic, emotional, musical and poetic. Not surprisingly, then, these superphysical perceptions are arranged in the form of poetic mantras. It's important to recognize that this form of communication is entirely contrary to Rudolf Steiner's deliberately-preferred usual method. In order to establish anthroposophy as an authentic spiritual science, Steiner deliberately conveyed spiritual knowledge in clear, concise, dispassionate intellectual concepts that could be cognitively understood and objectively verified. The mantras of the nineteen lessons are a profoundly-significant exception to Steiner's usual rule of spiritual communication.

It is also clear from the brief quotation on the previous page that the three Classes of the School of Spiritual Science are not intended to establish a new path of initiation.[46] There are no instructions or exercises given to separate the soul from the body in order to cross the threshold into the spiritual world. The lessons and Classes of the School are best described as a "meditative path" of imaginatively entering the spiritual world for non-initiates.

In other words, the purpose and intent of the Classes of the School of Spiritual Science is to mentally and emotionally *prepare* the esoteric student for what spiritual life is like on the other side of the threshold; as well as what is likely to consciously occur during the out-of-body experiences of sleep, death and initiation. When one acknowledges that this is the overall goal of the School Classes, then one can reasonable conclude that the Second and Third Classes would sequentially deepen and expand this esoteric meditative preparation of experiencing the spiritual world.

While the previous quotation doesn't explicitly state it, the lessons of the School of Spiritual Science are also to reflect and conform to the esoteric teachings that St. Michael gave in the spiritual world at the beginning of the fifteenth and nineteenth centuries. These teachings of the supersensible School of Michael formed the basis of anthroposophy and the School of Spiritual Science. As explained by Rudolf Steiner in a lecture given on 28 July 1924 entitled "The New

Age of Michael":

> Thus we have a double super-sensible preparation for what is to become Anthroposophy on the earth. We have the preparation in the great super-sensible School [of Michael] from the 15th century onward, and then we have what I have described as an Imaginative cult or ritual (*Cultus*) that took shape in the super-sensible at the end of the 18th and beginning of the 19th century, when all that the Michael pupils had learned in the super-sensible School before, was cast into mighty pictures and Imaginations. Thus were the souls prepared, who afterwards descended into the physical world, being destined through all these preparations to feel the inner impulse to seek for what would work as Anthroposophy on earth. (Published in *Karmic Relationships: Esoteric Studies—Volume III*; 2009)

In summary, then, any modern-day effort to continue the unfinished Classes of the School of Spiritual Science must take into consideration the aforementioned determinants. Not widely known among present-day anthroposophists is that there have been fairly-recent attempts to encourage the formation of a Second Class. In 1993, for instance, this idea was promoted in a conference program for members of the School of Spiritual Science by Manfred Schmidt-Brabant (1926–2001), the Chair of the Executive Council at that time. In spite of a popular interest among anthroposophists at the conference, no Second Class was forthcoming as a result.

When contemplating the possibility of augmenting the First Class or formulating a Second Class it is extremely unlikely that Steiner's mantric format could be continued. This is because it is based on describing highly-advanced supersensible perceptions: Imaginations, Inspirations and Intuitions. As a bodhisattva, Rudolf Steiner's clairvoyant ability was so supernally developed that it would take an equally-developed bodhisattva to augment his mantric lessons.

Nevertheless, if the purpose of the Class lessons is to increasingly prepare non-initiate School members for the experience of crossing the threshold into the spiritual world in full consciousness, then this further preparation doesn't have to be exclusively in mantric form.

It's quite possible, then, for a qualified individual to provide additional information on crossing the threshold, from their own supersensible experience, that would positively augment what has already been conveyed by Rudolf Steiner in the nineteen lessons of the First Class. This author's own account of personally crossing the threshold into the spiritual world under the guidance of Christ-Jesus—which has been published in *Following Christ Across the Threshold: The Non-Initiate's Guide to Entering the Spiritual World* (2019)—is one such recent attempt at formulating a potential Second Class.[47]

Of course any such attempt is bound at first to meet with mild to hostile resistance from anthroposophists who are suspicious of any addition to, or expansion of, Rudolf Steiner's work. Nevertheless, while a healthy skepticism and the need for intellectual scrutiny and validation are certainly expected with spiritual science, this should not inhibit open-minded anthroposophists from carefully considering any new contributions to Rudolf Steiner's work.

3.3.2 Integrating the Ego-Replica of Rudolf Steiner Will Help Renew Anthroposophy in the 21st Century

The more present-day anthroposophists begin to consciously and unconsciously integrate an ego-replica of Rudolf Steiner, the more anthroposophy will be positively renewed in the 21st century. This is because those individuals who intra-psychically bear a replica of Rudolf Steiner's ego-self are able to directly experience present-day events from Steiner's point of view. In other words, they have a strong internal sense of what Rudolf Steiner's moral position would be on particular happenings today.

This of course will help guide present-day anthroposophists with assessing and evaluating which changes or initiatives are consistent with Rudolf Steiner's intentions—which ones are right or wrong, good or bad, positive or negative from Steiner's point of view.

When anthroposophic gadfly Thomas Meyer (b.1950) published his version of Rudolf Steiner's nineteen lessons—entitled *The First Class Lessons and Mantras: The Michael School Meditative Path in Nineteen Steps* (2017)—he "felt compelled" to tweak the lessons by removing the introductory remarks about the School and the Christmas Conference, and placing them in a separate section at the back of his book. He explained his "compulsion" to create a new title and to "excise the separate talks" from the lessons as follows:

> The editor is of the opinion that this editorial decision is in harmony with the current intentions of the continuously working individuality of Rudolf Steiner.

While Meyer, in this case, acknowledges the need to be "in harmony" with Rudolf Steiner when changing or advancing anthroposophical teachings, on what basis has he determined "the current intentions" of Rudolf Steiner? The best way to do that in the 21st century is to integrate an ego-replica of Rudolf Steiner. As well, it is the current availability of Steiner's ego-replicas that best demonstrate that the "individuality of Rudolf Steiner" is "continuously working" today.

3.4 The General Anthroposophical Society Continues its Mission as an Esoteric Institution

Due to the unfortunate squabbling that has periodically broken out since Rudolf Steiner's death, some breakaway anthroposophists have mistakenly concluded that the General Anthroposophical Society no longer exists as an esoteric institution. This drastic, ill-conceived notion is simplistically based on the premise that the leaders and members of a truly esoteric society wouldn't quarrel amongst themselves—if they did, then the esoteric society would cease to exist.

It's difficult to believe how anyone truly familiar with anthroposophical history could arrive at such a hasty and erroneous conclusion. For one thing, by deliberately bringing together the karmically-feuding Platonists and Aristotelians in a desperate attempt to unite them in a shared spiritual mission, the General Anthroposophical Society fully expected that there would be some occasional, deep-seated internal conflict amongst members.

Besides, while the General Anthroposophical Society is an open and public institution with an esoteric centre and supernatural sponsors, it has still been established on earth to included the involvement of imperfect human beings in its guidance and direction. Consequently, it's to be expected that mistakes might well be made; but human imperfection is hardly a reason for such a divinely-appointed esoteric institution to cease to exist.

Furthermore, as a profoundly-important, Christ-centred spiritual institution, it should come as no surprise that the General Anthroposophical Society would come under serious demonic attack on occasion—internally, as well as externally.[48] These diabolical powers characteristically stir up strife and discord in an attempt to destroy spiritual endeavors such as anthroposophy.[49] Once again, it should come as no surprise that serious conflict has periodically occurred within the General Anthroposophical Society; but that benevolent spiritual powers have not allowed internal dissention to destroy the Society.[50]

Time and time again Rudolf Steiner emphasized that anthroposophy was an initiative of the spiritual world—more specifically, a Christ-inspired endeavor of St. Michael. Moreover, St. Michael had spent over four centuries establishing the supersensible Michael-School as preparation for anthroposophy on earth. It's rather astonishing to think that St. Michael—the preeminent warrior of light—would passively permit some internal squabbling to dissolve the General Anthroposophical Society.

Similarly, the esoteric establishment of the General Anthroposophical Society was also inspired and sponsored by the bodhisattvas of the West: Christian Rosenkreutz and Master Zarathas. Both exalted masters had initially worked with H. P. Blavatsky to found the Theosophical Society as the first, publically-registered esoteric society in world-history. Reluctantly, they were forced to abandon the Theosophical Society after it was surreptitiously hijacked by unscrupulous initiates in India for entirely political and nationalistic reasons.

Once again, it's incredulous to think that after successfully inspiring and sponsoring the General Anthroposophical Society—after so much difficulty—that Christian Rosenkreutz and Master Zarathas would just up and abandon the Society because of some periodic, internal (often juvenile), quibbling and bickering.

Prior to Rudolf Steiner's death in 1925, there had already erupted some serious divisions amongst anthroposophists. An understandably-exasperated Steiner actually considered for a time the idea of abandoning the Society; but wisely decided otherwise. Instead, he conjoined the anthroposophical movement and the Anthroposophical Society into one overarching organization with a centralized leadership and himself as the first president. He additionally established the School of Spiritual Science and authorized the construction of a second Goetheanum to function as an esoteric university for the School; and as the world-headquarters for the newly-established and spiritually-unifying General Anthroposophical Society.

According to Rudolf Steiner, conjoining the spiritual-scientific research of the anthroposophical movement with the bureaucratic-administrative functions of an esoteric society incurred some very serious risk. The supernal sources of spiritual-scientific knowledge might have decided to withdraw their activity. Happily instead, they decided to continue and even increase their revelatory activity within the new context of the General Anthroposophical Society.

In other words, Rudolf Steiner's sacrificial decision to heal the divisions within anthroposophy through the formation of the General Anthroposophical Society met with an overwhelming endorsement from the spiritual world. This being the case, it is extremely unlikely that the spiritual patrons of supersensible knowledge would easily undo their mentorship of the General Anthroposophical Society after Steiner's death, just because of some all-too-expected human frailty and immaturity on occasion.

In summation, then, disregarding what some breakaway anthroposophists have erroneously alleged, the General Anthroposophical Society has continued to exist—without interruption— since its initial formation in 1923-24; despite instances of poor leadership and diabolical attacks from within and without. Furthermore, since sincere anthroposophists (especially members of the School of Spiritual Science) are morally expected to represent, promote and defend anthroposophy in the world, whenever there is division or strife within the General Anthroposophical Society, they are certainly not expected to simply abandon the Society. Instead, they are expected to represent, promote and defend anthroposophy *within* the Society as well. In order to positively renew anthroposophy in the 21st century, anthroposophists need to recognize the importance of working *within* the General Anthroposophical Society; and *not external* to it.

CHAPTER 4

THE SPIRITUAL BATTLE OF THE 21ST CENTURY

4.1 The School of Spiritual Science: Rosicrucian Training of Michael's Warriors of Light

AS PREVIOUSLY MENTIONED, the School of Spiritual Science is the earthly reflection of a profound supersensible school of instruction that was conducted by St. Michael at the beginning of the fifteenth and nineteenth centuries. For that reason, Rudolf Steiner often referred to the School of Spiritual Science as the "Michael-School" or the "School of Michael."

Moreover, as a Christ-centred, Western school of esotericism, the School of Michael is naturally associated with the Rosicrucian Fraternity, since Christian Rosenkreutz is one of the bodhisattvas of the West. As stated by Rudolf Steiner near the end of a recapitulated Class Lesson that he gave on 6 September 1924:

> These are the words of the Michael-School. When they
> are spoken, Michael's spirit flows in waves through the

room in which they are spoken. And his sign is what confirms his presence.

Then Michael leads us to the real Rosicrucian School, which shall reveal the secrets of humanity in the past, in the present and in the future through the Father-God, the Son-God and the Spirit-God. And then pressing the seal on the words "rosae et crucis," the words may be pronounced:

- Ex deo nascimur
- In Christo morimur
- Per spiritum sanctum reviviscimus

4.1.1 Spiritualizing the Human Intellect in the Michael-School

While the Class lessons of the Michael-School are clearly designed to mentally and emotionally prepare non-initiate students to consciously cross the threshold into the spiritual world, the School itself has the broader goal of spiritualizing the human intellect. This is because St. Michael is esoterically known as the "great defender of cosmic intelligence."

As the power of intellectual thought became increasingly available to developing humanity—beginning in the Graeco-Roman cultural era—it also began to be exclusively directed toward the physical world. By the mid-nineteenth century, intellectual thought was in danger of becoming entirely materialistic and terrestrial; that is, under the complete control of dark Ahrimanic beings.

In order to prevent the entire "Ahrimanization" of intellectual thought, the legions of St. Michael fought and defeated a horde of Ahrimanic beings during the second-half of the nineteenth century. Thankfully, this victory safeguarded and increased the ability for human beings to access and comprehend the spiritual world through intellectual thought. The School of Spiritual Science is St. Michael's continuing effort to assist struggling mankind in spiritualizing intellectual thought.

4.1.2 Preparing Warriors of Light in the Michael-School

Most esotericists and Christians recognize St. Michael the Archangel as the great warrior of light who has heroically fought and prevailed against the "dragon" of Ahrimanic-Satanic beings throughout history on behalf of vulnerable humanity. Of course St. Michael is not alone in this ongoing battle; but commands vast legions of celestial beings loyal to Christ-Jesus and faithful to God.

Furthermore, human beings are also provided with the stupendous opportunity to assist St. Michael and his legions of light in the spiritual battle of the 21st century. In the School of Spiritual Science—for those who freely volunteer—St. Michael himself will supersensibly prepare warrior-souls for spiritual battle. Armed with the sword of spiritual truth and the shield of moral righteousness, students of the Michael-School can make a significant contribution to assisting St. Michael in his defense of mankind.

So, how best can members of the School assist St. Michael in his 21st century battle against the Ahrimanic dragon? The most obvious way is to put into daily practice exactly what the Michael-School has been designed to accomplish—the spiritualization of intellectual thought. However, even though anthroposophists have been taught that "thinking is a spiritual activity,"[51] many don't fully realize that a clash of ideas is quite literally a spiritual battle.

Unfortunately today, the world is awash in falsehood, lies, propaganda, disinformation, deception, materialism, secularism, atheism, communism, fearfulness, uncertainty, delusions, egotism, narcissism, emotionalism, immorality, illogic, hatred, violence, terrorism and manipulation. The only way of not becoming submerged in this tsunami of Ahrimanic and Luciferic mind-control is to mentally focus on the spiritual truth—that is, to spiritualize intellectual thought.

While this may be easy to say, it certainly isn't easy to do. Since the present-day flood of anti-spiritual mentation is ultimately generated and directed by nefarious beings much more powerful than ordinary human beings, when anthroposophists are engaged in this spiritual battle on the plane of mental ideation, assistance from more powerful celestial beings of light (truth) is critically necessary.

The most powerful and effective ally in the spiritual battle of truth versus falsehood is of course Christ-Jesus. By hypostatically uniting the human nature of Jesus with the divine nature of God the Son, Christ-Jesus is able to embody and personify divine Truth; and to openly declare: "I AM the Truth" (John 14:6). As anthroposophists, by intra-psychically uniting with Christ-Jesus, the divine-spirit of Truth becomes internalized and actively involved in determining spiritual truth from diabolical falsehood.

For this reason, St. Michael—the "Countenance of Christ"— in his School of Spiritual Science, will always direct student-members' attention to Christ-Jesus. Using the spiritual-scientific method of studying and comprehending the "Mysteries of the Son" that are embodied in Christ-Jesus, St. Michael can effectively spiritualize intellectual thought; which is critically necessary in order to win the spiritual battle of the 21st century.

4.2 Recognizing the Rise of Sorath and the New Triad of Evil

In any prolonged battle, whether physical or spiritual, it is always strategically wise to know your enemy as much as possible. Consequently, the anthroposophical foot-soldiers trained in the School of Michael need to thoroughly recognize and understand the principal perpetrators of supernatural evil.

The spiritual battle of the 21st century has taken on a new and more dangerous configuration with the additional involvement of another powerful perpetrator of supernatural evil. Up to Rudolf Steiner's time, the principal supernatural adversaries of humanity since the ancient Lemurian Age have been Lucifer and Ahriman. However, since 1933, a third evil opponent—Sorath—has become increasingly involved.[52] Previously, mankind struggled against a duality of evil; from now on, mankind must struggle against a triad of evil instead.[53]

This modern-day triad of evil is a corrupt inversion of the divine Trinity: Ahriman is the infernal debasement of the Father; Lucifer is the infernal debasement of the Holy Spirit;[54] and Sorath is the infernal debasement of the Son (see Figure 2 below).

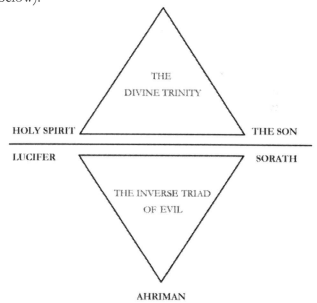

Figure 2: The Inverse Triad of Evil

By taking the positive and beneficial universal forces of the divine Trinity to an extreme degree, the triad of evil perpetrators distort, debase and corrupt their true purpose and activity. More specifically, by taking the universal forces of expansion and proliferation to an extreme degree, Lucifer perverts the activity of the Holy Spirit. Likewise, by taking the universal forces of contraction and centralization to an extreme degree, Ahriman perverts the activity of the Father. And by taking the universal forces of balance and equilibrium to an extreme degree, Sorath perverts the activity of the Son.

By misapplying the universal forces of the Father, Ahriman strives to congeal and densify the spiritual realm down to the physical; thereby condensing mankind down to animalistic man-machines on earth—under his control. Contrarily, by misapplying the universal forces of the Holy Spirit, Lucifer strives to rarify, over-expand and hyper-inflate the physical realm out into the cosmos; thereby transporting mankind up into a false dream-world of delusion and fantasy—under his control. Sorath, on the other hand, by corrupting the universal forces of the Son, seeks to cause chaos, havoc and confusion between the physical and spiritual realms; thereby dissociating mankind into individuated, self-seeking, blood-thirsty savages—under his control.

4.2.1 The Duality of Evil and the Hermetic Principle of Polarity

When the evil adversaries of mankind manifested as a duality, as in Rudolf Steiner's time, one of the principal methods of neutralizing the harmful effects of Lucifer and Ahriman was to apply the "Hermetic principle of polarity"; which states:

> Everything is dual; everything has poles; everything has its pair of opposites; like and unlike are the same; opposites

are identical in nature, but different in degree; extremes meet; all truths are but half-truths; all paradoxes may be reconciled. (*The Kybalion: A Study of the Hermetic Philosophy of Ancient Egypt and Greece*; 1940)

A commonplace example of applying the Hermetic principle of polarity is in the case of hot and cold. Hot and cold are polar opposites on a spectrum of warmth energy: "hot" being a high degree of warmth energy; and "cold" being a low degree of warmth energy. If a room, for instance, is too cold, then it can be made more temperately neutral by increasing the hot pole of the spectrum according to the Hermetic principle of polarity.

Similarly with Lucifer and Ahriman, who often manifest as polar opposites. Lucifer, for example, incites hot-headed over-reaction in individuals which causes their thoughts and emotions to temporarily "fly off." Ahriman, on the other hand, instills cold, hard-headed intellection in individuals which causes a rigidification of their thinking and a stultification of their emotions. By applying the Hermetic principle of polarity, Luciferic hot-headedness can be cooled down by invoking Ahrimanic hard-headedness. Likewise, Ahrimanic frigidity can be fired up by invoking Luciferic fervency.[55]

While the extremes of Lucifer and Ahriman can certainly be held in check, neutralized and balanced by applying the Hermetic principle of polarity, there is enormous risk for human beings to play off one powerful evil-adversary against the other. Obviously, this is better left to a more powerful, God-ordained being such as Christ-Jesus. For that reason, human efforts to balance the extremes of Lucifer and Ahriman are much safer and more effective if one is in spiritual union with Christ-Jesus. Rudolf Steiner artistically conveyed this idea in his sculpture entitled, "The Representative of Man," as shown in Figure 3 on the next page.

Figure 3: "The Representative of Man"
(Christ Balancing Lucifer and Ahriman)[56]

4.2.2 Rectifying the Triad of Evil with the Divine Forces of the Trinity

Since the triad of evil—Lucifer, Ahriman and Sorath—is a diabolical inversion of the divine Trinity, it makes logical sense that the infernal actions of the triad can be counteracted and rectified by the supernal power of the Trinity; once again, by applying the Hermetic principle of polarity.

So for example, the luciferic exaggeration of the universal forces of expansion and proliferation can be corrected by invoking the divine contractive power of the Father. Likewise, Ahriman's distortion of the universal forces of contraction and centralization can be corrected by invoking the divine expansive power of the Holy Spirit. And Sorath's corruption of the universal forces of equilibrium and balance can be corrected by the divine, harmonization power of the Son (please refer to Figure 4 on the next page).

4.2.3 Transforming the Exaggerated Forces of the Evil Triad through the Centralization of Christ-Jesus

Somewhat similar to invoking the divine power of the Trinity in order to rectify the iniquitous exaggeration of universal forces by the triad of evil is to place Christ-Jesus at the centre of all human life and world evolution.

Since Christ-Jesus—through his sacrificial death, resurrection and ascension—has overcome and vanquished Lucifer, Ahriman and Sorath in his own life, he is now able to assist others to do the same. Even though Christ-Jesus has personally triumphed over the triad of evil, he does not force his momentous achievement on other human beings. To do so would seriously impinge on individual free-will. Our Saviour's victory can be shared; but only if individuals freely choose to spiritually unite with him.

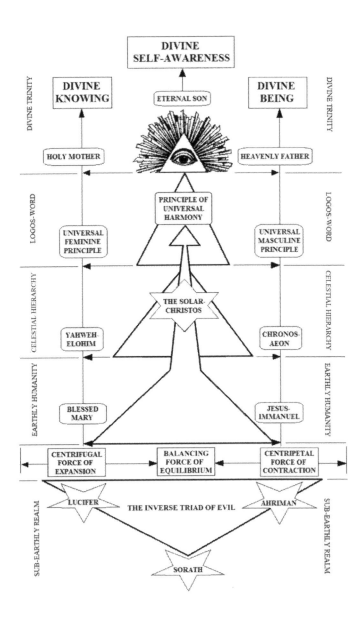

Figure 4: The Universal Principle of Triplicity[57]

As individuals, by placing Christ-Jesus at the centre of our being, from there he's able to draw on the harmonizing power of the Son in order to overcome and to balance the inverse triad of evil. As similarly stated by Rudolf Steiner in a lecture given on 18 May 1915:

> Rather, everything that man has to strive for as a result of the Christ impulse must be seen as similar to the equilibrious state of a pendulum. In the center, the pendulum is in perfect balance, but it must oscillate to one side or the other. The same applies to man's development here on earth. Man must oscillate to the one side according to the luciferic principle and to the other according to the principle of Ahriman, but he must maintain his equilibrium through the cultivation of Paul's declaration, "Not I, but Christ in me." (Published in *Christ in Relation to Lucifer and Ahriman*; 1978)

4.3 Acknowledging the Destined Incarnation of Ahriman as the Antichrist

For the 21st-century student-warriors of St. Michael in the School of Spiritual Science, it's imperative to recognize and to prepare for the possibly-impending incarnation of Ahriman as the prophesized Antichrist.[58] Since much of the social, economic, political and religious turmoil occurring in the 21st century world today can be attributed to, and seen as preparation for, the destined incarnation of the Antichrist, it's imperative for St. Michael's legions on earth to acknowledge this in order to counteract and resist the increasing spread.

While the Bible, being a Christian document, was the first to mention the "Antichrist," it is scant on providing any specific detail. Furthermore, what little is provided is entirely from St. John the evangelist; as in the following New Testament passages:

Little children, it is the last hour: and as you have heard that Antichrist cometh, even now there are become many Antichrists: whereby we know that it is the last hour. (1 John 2:18).

Many deceivers have gone out into the world, those who do not confess that Jesus Christ has come in the flesh; any such person is the deceiver and the antichrist! (2 John 1:7)

Who is the liar but the one who denies that Jesus is the Christ? This is the antichrist, the one who denies the Father and the Son. (1 John 2:22)

By this you know the Spirit of God: every spirit that confesses that Jesus Christ has come in the flesh is from God, and every spirit that does not confess Jesus is not from God. And this is the spirit of the antichrist, of which you have heard that it is coming; and now it is already in the world. (1 John 4:2–3)

Though this is the extent of biblical references to the Antichrist, the Catholic Church and various leaders within the Church have added more specific detail; such as the following:

The supreme religious deception is that of the Antichrist, a pseudo-messianism by which man glorifies himself in place of God and of his Messiah come in the flesh. (Paragraph 675 of the *Catechism of the Catholic Church*)

The Antichrist will not be so called; otherwise he would have no followers. He will not wear red tights, nor vomit sulphur, nor carry a trident nor wave an arrowed tail as Mephistopheles in *Faust*. This masquerade has helped the Devil convince men that he does not exist.

[H]e will come disguised as the Great Humanitarian; he will talk peace, prosperity and plenty not as means to lead us to God, but as ends in themselves ...

He will tempt Christians with the same three temptations with which he tempted Christ ...

[H]e will have one great secret which he will tell to no one: he will not believe in God. Because his religion will be brotherhood without the fatherhood of God, he will deceive even the elect. He will set up a counterchurch ... It will have all the notes and characteristics of the Church, but in reverse and emptied of its divine content. It will be a mystical body of the Antichrist that will in all externals resemble the mystical body of Christ. (Venerable Fulton J. Sheen (1895–1979); *Communism and the Conscience of the West*, 1948)

Familiar to anthroposophists is the esoteric knowledge that St. John the evangelist—the biblical source of information about the Antichrist—in a subsequent incarnation, became known as Christian Rosenkreutz, the founder of the Rosicrucian Fraternity. It is perhaps no surprise then, that the most esoteric information ever publically revealed about the Antichrist has come from eminent Rosicrucian initiate, Rudolf Steiner.

For instance, the spiritual-scientific research of Rudolf Steiner has confirmed the longstanding Christian tradition that the Antichrist will be a physical incarnation of Satan (Ahriman) that is unavoidably destined to occur. Steiner's research goes on to reveal that the incarnation of Ahriman will occur somewhere in the West, and sometime during the third millennium.[59] In addition, it's predicted that Ahriman will establish a powerful occult institution that will provide easy access to a subjective, pseudo-clairvoyance for everyone;[60] as well as enhanced physical intellection by ingesting occultly-derived, supplemental nutrients.

Since it is extremely unlikely that a powerful supernatural being such as Ahriman would incarnate as a human child, the more logical prediction is that he will take possession of a willing adult-host; and thereby avoid the unproductive years of physical maturation. In this regard, the most likely age of adult possession is from 30 to 33 years-old. Christian esotericists have also feared that since there is a significant outpouring of Ahrimanic activity and influencing every 666 years—1998 (ie: 3 x 666 years)—would be a propitious time for a possible incarnation of Ahriman.

Since no charismatic individual fitting the description of the Antichrist noticeably entered upon the world stage in 1998, it can be reasonably concluded that Ahriman did not incarnate at that time. However, it's quite possible that his chosen human-host was born during that year; in which case Ahriman's incarnation could still occur as early as 2028 (ie: 1998 + 30).

Even though Ahriman has until the year 3000 to incarnate, he intends to incarnate as early as possible, so as to better surprise and take advantage of an unprepared humanity. The Christ-imbued legions of St. Michael, on the other hand, are engaged in delaying Ahriman's inevitable incarnation for as long as possible in order to enable mankind to best prepare for their thoroughly-evil and totally-unwelcomed supernatural "guest."

As well as strategically considering the advantageous element of surprise, Ahriman and his evil-cohorts are also actively engaged in shaping particular earthly events from the superphysical realm in an effort to make his physical incarnation as diabolically smooth and successful as possible. Consequently, it's imperative that St. Michael's loyal recruits on earth heed, inform and resist Ahriman's preparatory machinations; in order to make his incarnation as difficult as possible.

4.4 Opposing the Diabolical Forces of the New World Order

No doubt the most effective and easiest way for Ahriman to completely control the world when he incarnates is for a one-world totalitarian government to be already established. That way, Ahriman—using his vast occult ability and his computer-like intellectual cunning—will simply appoint himself the head of the world government; and thereby control the global-levers of power.

With this in mind, it should come as no surprise that much of the inexplicable turmoil that has been globally occurring throughout the first decades of the 21st century is being caused by attempts to establish a sinister one-world government—popularly known as the "New World Order."

4.4.1 The Rise of Radical-Socialism in the West

One such example is the pernicious spread of radical-socialist ideology throughout the Western nations. Despite the historical evidence that radically-socialist (and communist) regimes have repeatedly failed over time, it is still infecting Western culture—"Why is that?"

As an atheistic ideology, radical-socialism seeks to replace the supremacy of God with the supremacy of the State. Instead of persons being regarded as uniquely-individual children of God; radical-socialism regards each citizen as an unimportant, dispensable "cog" in the all-controlling, political "machinery" of the State. Radical-socialism characteristically imposes a pernicious and unnatural form of "equality" on everyone and everything within the almighty State (except on the controlling elite, of course). Rather than guaranteeing an incentivizing "equality of opportunity" for everyone; the State forcibly imposes a soul-numbing "equality of outcome" on everyone instead.

In order to reduce everyone to the same dull outcome level, the radical-socialist State forcibly "dumbs-down" individual excellence; as well as merited reward for innovation, hard-work, innate talent or expertise. Every personal incentive is reduced to an equal level of bland mediocrity. As historically proven, the sinister rationale for enforcing a State-wide equality of outcome on everyone, is because a general population that is compliantly docile is obviously much easier to control and direct.

4.4.2 The Radical-Socialist Effort to Weaken a Strong America

In order to establish a one-world socialist government, all nations must be forcibly "equalized" in compliance with the radical-socialist tenet of equality of outcome. Accordingly, one nation can't be more militarily stronger, or economically wealthier, or technologically superior, or educationally smarter, or more culturally dominant, or more religiously homogeneous than any other.

Consequently, as the world's only remaining super-power, the United States is a major obstacle in establishing a global, super-socialist State. Therefore, it is imperative that the United States be drastically weakened economically, militarily, culturally, educationally, technologically and religiously. This explains why globalist and radical-socialist forces have been seriously targeting the United States for the past three decades.

Under the eight presidential years from 2009 to 2017 of devious closet-socialist, Barak Hussein Obama, the United States was severely weakened by the globalist and socialist elites.[61] No doubt, if "crooked" Hilary Clinton had become his presidential successor, American prominence and preeminence as a world superpower would have been seriously compromised and weakened. As a nefarious result, there would have been no American opposition to the radical-socialist plan to install Communist China as the leading economic-driver in the New World Order.[62]

Unfortunately for the architects of the New World Order, Donald J. Trump soundly defeated Hilary Clinton for the US presidency in 2016. President Trump immediately halted and began reversing the subversive momentum of the radical-socialists to weaken America. Trump's wildly-popular election slogan: "Make America Great Again"—was anathema to the radical-socialists; and an "existential threat" to their devious plan for world-takeover. As a result, the radical-left has declared all-out war on US President Trump.

This all-out war against Trump has revealed just how pervasive, pernicious and infectious the influence of radical-socialism has become in America. In order to mount a full-scale assault on President Trump, the agents of radical-socialism in America were forced to come out of hiding for all to see. It's clearly obvious now that the Democratic Party has been completely hijacked by radical-socialist forces.

Similarly with most of the mainstream media; where once they were merely biased toward the left, now they are entirely-untruthful, fake-news propaganda mills for radical-socialism. The morally-depraved Hollywood elites have also exhibited a longstanding left-wing bias; but now display a rabidly-socialist culture and mindset. A great many American universities have revealed themselves to be nothing more than indoctrination centres for Marxist-communist ideology.

The scientific and medical communities have also betrayed their supposed objectivity and neutrality by openly promoting the radical-socialist agenda on pro-abortion activism, gender theory, gender re-assignment surgery, fetal-tissue research and anthropogenic global warming (AGW).

4.4.3 The Radical-Socialist Attack on Religion, Particularly Christianity

Not surprisingly, as an atheistic, Godless ideology, radical-socialism (communism) is vehemently opposed to religious freedom and to the open practice of religion. In communist countries, if religion can't be stamped out completely; then it is put under State control instead (as in present-day Communist China). This has also been occurring in the United States today.

This became particularly obvious during the recent Wuhan virus pandemic. The radical-socialist, Democratic governors and mayors openly discriminated against religious institutions. For example, in the early stages of the pandemic, the governors of California, Alaska, Washington, New York, Idaho, Montana, Minnesota, Illinois, and Vermont all banned religious gatherings; but kept liquor stores (and in some cases, pot stores) open for business.

Since religious faiths and institutions are generally opposed to an atheist ideology such as radical-socialism or communism, they naturally stand in the way of the New World Order. Christianity—particularly the Catholic Church—is the greatest threat because it is an international institution with 1.33 billion members (in 2018). This is why radical-socialist multi-billionaire, George Soros, has formed an alliance made in hell with socialist Pope Francis.

Soros has infiltrated the hallowed halls of the Vatican with longtime operatives such as economist and notorious population-control advocate, Jeffrey Sachs. Sachs is also infamously known as the chief architect of the U.N.'s Sustainable Development Goals (SDGs). He is also known to be a strong supporter of radical-socialist Democratic Bernie Sanders; and is a vehement critic of the Trump administration for "threatening multilateralism." Sachs has managed to weasel his way into becoming a papal advisor on "sustainable development"; that is on the U.N.'s socialist agenda.

Prior to Pope Francis, conservative and traditionalist Popes St. John Paul II and Benedict XVI soundly rejected socialism, communism and humanism as completely contrary to established Catholic Faith. Francis, on the other hand, has wholeheartedly embraced these anti-Catholic ideologies; and is consequently regarded by many in the Church as an anti-Pope who is endeavoring to institute a radical-socialist anti-Church.

4.4.4 The Globalist Agenda to Centralize Control of the World's Economy

Another key component to establish a one-world, socialist super-State (the New World Order) is to gain centralized control of the world's money supply. To this end, as far back as 1943 globalist forces established international financial institutions such as the World Bank and the International Monetary Fund (IMF). In addition, every developed country on earth has established a centralized national bank to control the money supply and to regulate the country's economy.

What many people are not aware of is that there is also an international central bank for the national central banks that's located in Basel, Switzerland, called the Bank for International Settlements (BIS). This global financial overseer aims to "promote" (ie: control) global monetary and financial stability.

At present, each national central bank is only allowed to print its own country's currency; it cannot print another country's currency. While there is no single international currency officially instituted today, the US dollar often functions as the monetary unit of international trade and commerce. Nevertheless, certain international financial institutions such as the IMF and the BIS are now able to issue "Special Drawing Rights" (SDRs) as a form of global currency.

Up until the Great Depression of the 1930s, a nation's paper currency was backed by gold reserves. This system controlled the amount of new currency that a central bank could print. The central banks managed to get around that restriction by agreeing to discontinue using the gold standard. That way, central banks could literally print money out of nothing—termed "fiat money." In addition, commercial banks can lend out $9 for every $1 that they receive from the central bank; thereby creating more money out of nothing through the "money multiplier" effect. Furthermore, in today's technological world, more and more money is simply a digital credit or debit amount.

While the current international, centralized banking system still appears to be under the control of several national governments, certain globalist elites long to have it under the control of a worldwide, socialist super-State government (the New World Order).

4.4.5 Using a Worldwide Existential Threat as a Reason to Establish a One-World Government

Radical-socialists have long understood that otherwise freedom-loving people are more than willing to give up their fundamental civil rights and cherished freedoms to centralized governmental control when faced with a real or perceived existential threat—such as war, famine, disease or natural disaster.

Knowing this, since 2001 the covert architects of the New World Order have used three global threats to further advance their nefarious agenda: (1) the war on terrorism, (2) anthropogenic global warming (AGW), and (3) the Wuhan virus pandemic.

The radical-Moslem terrorist attack on the Twin Towers in New York on September 11, 2001, provided ultra-right wing forces within the administration of President George W. Bush with a golden opportunity to seriously curtail some fundamental human rights and freedoms in America and abroad. For example, the introduction of the Patriot Act just weeks after the terrorist attack (October 26, 2001) provided

US intelligence agencies with the legal rationale to spy on American citizens, to impose widespread camera surveillance, to monitor phone calls and internet activity, to employ new methods of torture overseas, to set up secret prison-camps on foreign soil, to detain citizens indefinitely without arrest, and to search and seize private property without judicial approval.

Furthermore, the war on terrorism was easily used psychologically to incite widespread fear in the general public, since terrorism was treated as an invisible threat. Terrorists could be anyone, found anywhere, with the ability to strike at any time. The war on terrorism also provided American war-hawks with a feeble excuse to militarily invade Afghanistan and Iraq (even though the Twin Tower terrorists were largely Saudi Arabian).

Over time, as international coalition forces began to successfully curtail Islamic terrorists, a new global threat had to be found that would unite the world's nations in a common enemy. The contrived global threat that superseded the war on terrorism was "anthropogenic global warming" (AGW); otherwise known as man-made climate change. Amazingly, in many ways, climate change alarmism has proved to be even more effective at inducing worldwide fear and panic. As incredible as it seems, a decades-long, worldwide barrage of pseudo-scientific propaganda has fearfully convinced vast numbers of people today that the earth could actually end as early as 2030.

The fear of Islamic terrorism didn't come anywhere near this level of irrational fearfulness. The only thing that came close to this level of global, apocalyptic fearfulness was the nuclear arms race during the 1950s and 60s. However, in that case, the fear of nuclear annihilation was real and justified. In the case of man-made climate change, the imminent threat is fraudulent and contrived. For that reason, truthful scientific research is slowly chipping away at the phony, factual foundations of the global-warming, end-times house of cards.

Increasing numbers of people and nations are rejecting the hyperbolic propaganda.

Because of its decreasing effectiveness in advancing the one-world socialist super-State, climate change alarmism has been augmented by an additional experiment designed to test the most effective way to incite worldwide fear in order to gain total population control. That experiment was the Chinese release of the Wuhan virus in late-December, 2019.

From the perspective of the evil-proponents of the New World Order, the rapid spread of, and fearful reaction to, the Wuhan virus has been a tremendously successful experiment in worldwide population control. It was astonishing to think how quickly and how willingly the world's population and a multitude of nations agreed to forced, long-term lock-downs, social distancing and mask wearing, without any definitive scientific proof of effectiveness. What happened to the democratic right of assembly when individuals could be arrested for gathering on an open beach? What happened to the democratic right of religious worship when churches were forced to lock their doors?

It was disturbingly amazing how rapidly and pervasively a pandemic of fear spread across the globe concerning a virus that was only slightly more virulent than the regular flu virus. What was all too obvious was how different the virus was handled by radical-socialist politicians (such as Democrat governors and mayors in America) and conservative politicians (such as Republican governors and mayors in America). Leftist politicians quickly morphed into draconian "corona-Nazis"; issuing police-state regulations and assuming dictatorial control. If anyone had any doubts about how a really serious global pandemic could result in a one-world, socialist police-State, those doubts were shattered with the Wuhan virus.

In summary, it's abundantly clear to unbiased, critical observation that the raging political, social, economic and religious upheaval in America and abroad is not haphazard and unconnected; but is a coordinated and concerted attempt to establish a global, socialist super-State—the New World Order. The more that the legions of St. Michael on earth recognize and understand this, the better prepared they will be to resist, oppose and defeat this worldwide peril.

4.5 Christ-centred Protection and the Feminine Role of Blessed Mary in Opposing Evil

In the spiritual battle of the 21st century, it's crucial that anthroposophists continue to focus on the esoteric fact that the General Anthroposophical Society is an open and public branch of the Rosicrucian Fraternity. As such, it belongs to the stream of esoteric Christianity established by St. John the Beloved; and is therefore not a religion and theology, but a Christ-centred philosophy and theosophy.

It should be clear, then, that our foremost leader in this spiritual battle is Christ-Jesus; ably assisted by the celestial legions of St. Michael the Archangel. Most importantly as well, due to the hypostatic union of his human nature with the divine nature of God, Christ-Jesus can draw on the macrocosmic power of the Logos-Word, and the omnipotent power of the Son in this spiritual battle.

Understandably, talk of "warfare" and "battle" may not resonate with female anthroposophists. Nevertheless, aside from Christ-Jesus, the most powerful human defender against the perpetrators of evil is Blessed Mary, Queen of Heaven. In the words of Catholic mystic, Thomas à Kempis (1380–1471):

> The evil spirits greatly fear the Queen of Heaven, and flee at the sound of her name, as if from fire. At the very sound of the word Mary, they are cast down as if by thunder.

In Blessed Mary's case, she's not a Joan of Arc figure clad in shining armour and wielding a deadly sword. Instead, Mary's powerful opposition to the forces of evil is her radiating presence; that is, the moral goodness, pristine purity and the supernal love in her soul—that blazes outwardly as a flaming star of transcendent beauty.

Mary's supernal love even extends to the fallen spirits; who are sadly driven to flee from her by the force of *their own* internal evil. Unfortunately, the light of truth and the warmth of love are experienced by wicked spirits as fiery pain and suffering; causing them to take refuge in spiritual darkness.[63]

Due to Blessed Mary's shining example, female anthroposophists who don't envision themselves as "warriors" in St. Michael's earthy legions are still able to profoundly contribute in this struggle by visualizing themselves as bright torches of truth, beauty and goodness that repel supernatural evil, and light the difficult path to eventual victory.

CONCLUSION

CLEARLY, TO THE keen esoteric observer, these are crucial times in human history that St. Michael has long been preparing anthroposophists for in his School of Spiritual Science within the General Anthroposophical Society. Furthermore, these times call for a unity of purpose and action; not a multiple fracturing of independent "anthroposophical" initiatives (however well-meaning they might be).

It's also logically obvious that the divine, angelic and bodhisattva sponsors who fought so hard to established the General Anthroposophical Society as the first, Christ-centred, esoteric public society in human history, tenaciously continue to defend and infuse its sacred mission.

Neither is it logically reasonable to think that Rudolf Steiner would easily abandon the Society that he was so lovingly and sacrificially instrumental in creating—even after the separation of his death. To assist the Society's renewal and re-strengthening in the 21st century, Rudolf Steiner has compassionately offered up replications of his ego-vehicle that can be intimately united with the prepared souls of dedicated anthroposophists.

A strong and united General Anthroposophical Society is

critically needed on the side of the Christ-centred legions of light in the spiritual battle of the 21st century against the fallen spirits of darkness. The spiritualization of intellectual thinking is one of the strongest weapons that St. Michael has anthroposophically developed for use against the Ahrimanic dragon who is striving to incarnate as the destined Antichrist.

With the indwelling spirit of truth—Christ-Jesus—who can best spiritualize intellectual thought, the present-day diabolical machinations to establish a one-world, socialist super-State (the New World Order) as preparation for the Antichrist can be well-discerned and effectively resisted. This will help to prepare humanity to recognize and resist the false-messiah—Ahriman—when he physically incarnates to "prowl about the world, seeking the ruin of souls."[64]

NOTES

INTRODUCTION

1. A "Christian initiate" is one who follows the path of Esoteric-Christianity established by St. John the Evangelist; rather than the path of Exoteric-Christianity established by St. Peter the Apostle. Christian initiation involves the application and practice of special developmental exercises and techniques in order to unfold latent supersensible powers and abilities.

CHAPTER 1

2. Esoteric science recognizes that our Present-Earth Period of planetary evolution is divided into seven distinct ages:

   (1) The Polarian Age
   (2) The Hyperborean Age
   (3) the Lemurian Age
   (4) The Atlantean Age
   (5) The Age of Western Civilization
   (6) The Sixth Great Age

(7) The Seventh Great Age.

We are currently living in the second half of the Age of Western Civilization.

3. Esoteric science also maintains that our current Post-Atlantean Age is further sub-divided into seven cultural eras:

(1) The Ancient Indian cultural era
(2) The Ancient Persian cultural era
(3) The Egypto-Babylonian cultural era
(4) The Graeco-Roman cultural era
(5) The Anglo-Saxon-European cultural era
(6) The Future Slavic cultural era
(7) The Future American cultural era

We are currently living in the Anglo-Saxon-European cultural era.

4. According to clairvoyant investigation, there are a number of invisible, transcendent planes of existence beyond the physical. The transcendent plane that is closest to the physical world is known as the "etheric" realm.

5. Anthroposophists are aware that the soul of Gilgamesh later incarnated as Dr. Ita Wegman (1876–1943), a close personal friend and colleague of Rudolf Steiner.

6. Throughout ancient times, in several areas of the world, there existed highly-secretive institutions that jealously guarded advanced knowledge of the physical and spiritual realms.

   In ancient Greece, these institutions were known as Mystery schools or Mystery religions. Admittance was only granted after successfully passing a series of grueling physical and mental ordeals.

   After subsequent preparation, the successful candidate (or "initiate") was required to undergo the "temple sleep." With this ritual experience, the initiate was hypnotically placed in a death-like trance for three days, during which the soul was temporarily separated from the body, and free to sojourn in the superphysical realms.

Upon revival. The initiate was considered "reborn" as a "dweller in two worlds." All clairvoyantly-acquired knowledge obtained during the trance journey (called "gnosis") was kept within the strict confines of the Mystery school under penalty of death.

Despite their highly-secretive nature, Mystery schools were tremendously influential throughout ancient times in establishing the cultural practices of art, religion, education and politics. A great many prominent and leading figures during ancient times were initiates of a particular Mystery school.

7. This particular *Epic* detail strongly suggests that during his Mystery school initiatory-trance, the soul of Enkidu returned to the etheric world; but still continued to clairvoyantly communicate with Gilgamesh.

8. Lucifer, according to esoteric research, is a highly-developed celestial being who has stubbornly and selfishly chosen to oppose progressive human evolution. As such he is a formidable enemy of mankind who seeks to do evil.

9. Interestingly, anthroposophical information indicates that the soul of Gilgamesh also incarnated at this time as a female pupil of Cratylus known as Artemisia or "Mysa."

10. The eventual reconciliation between Platonists and Aristotelians in the late-twentieth century will be discussed in more detail in Chapter 3.

11. Rudolf Steiner's writings: books, plays, essays and poetry—are published in about forty volumes. The over 6000 recorded lectures that he gave make up another 300 volumes.

12. The legendary name of "Schionatulander" may not have been Steiner's actual historical name during this incarnation.

13. "Manichaeism" was a syncretic religion that combined elements of Christianity, Judaism, Zoroastrianism, Buddhism and Gnosticism. It was characterized by a complex, dualistic cosmology that postulated a universal struggle between a "good" spiritual world of light and an "evil" material world of darkness. Manichaeism thrived between the third and seventh centuries, and for a short time it was one of the world's most popular religions; but by the fourteenth century it had slowly died out.

14. One of the primary sources of evil opposition directed at the Knights of the Holy Grail was the notorious black magician known esoterically as Klingsor, the Duke of Terra de Labur in Calabria, Italy. Klingsor was also iniquitously allied with Moslem sorcerers secretly occupying a fortress in Sicily known as Calot Bobot. These Moslem magicians worshipped an evil goddess named Iblis who was diabolically opposed to the Holy Grail.

15. As extolled by English philosopher, G.K. Chesterton (1874–1936):

    It will not be possible to conceal much longer from anybody the fact that St. Thomas Aquinas was one of the great liberators of the human intellect. (*St. Thomas Aquinas*; 2011)

16. "St. Thomas did not reconcile Christ to Aristotle; he reconciled Aristotle to Christ" (G.K. Chesterton; Ibid).

17. During his day, St. Thomas argued against Platonic philosophy and its Christian supporters—such as St. Augustine of Hippo (354–430)—countering the belief that the natural world of the senses was inferior to the sublime world of eternal ideas; and therefore unworthy of intellectual study. St. Thomas also opposed Manichaean theology for adopting the gnostic belief that the material world was an evil manifestation not worthy of intellectual

consideration.

18. Anthroposophists are aware that Reginald of Piperno was a previous incarnation of the soul of Ita Wegman.

19. It's quite possible that this close brush with death was due to the supernatural forces evil; who very often attempt to prevent a high initiate from being born.

20. Rudolf Steiner's baptismal date has very often been used as his birth date. Apparently, this was a common practice among Catholics in the past; that is, to joyously celebrate the baptismal date as the "birth day of becoming Christian."

21. Most anthroposophists are aware that Karl Julius Schröer was previously incarnated as Plato. This of course explains the close karmic connection that Rudolf Steiner had with him at the Technische Hochschule. It also explains why Schröer was such a devoted Platonic Idealist at that time.

22. One particular supersensible perception mentioned by Goethe was his "archetypical plant," that was responsible for shaping the complete form—leaf, stem, blossom and root.

23. As stated by Steiner in his autobiography:

> What I had set forth, therefore, on the basis of Goethe's theory of the organic sent me afresh to the theory of knowledge ...

> I discovered that there was no theory of knowledge fitting Goethe's form of knowledge. This induced me to sketch, at least, such a theory. (*The Course of My Life*; 1986)

24. To be more esoterically accurate, thinking is an activity of the soul, as are feeling and willing. Thinking becomes a conscious spiritual activity with the realization that it is being generated by something superior to the mind—the higher ego, the real "I" or spiritual self. It isn't thinking,

then, that generates the ego of a person; it's the spiritual ego-self that generates and directs a person's thinking.

25. The Theosophical Society is an international organization that was founded in 1875 by Helena Petrovna Blavatsky, Colonel Henry Steel Olcott, William Quan Judge (and 16 others). The original headquarters is located in Adyar, India.

26. Some examples of Rosicrucian references in Goethe's poem, *The Mysteries*, are the following:

> He feels anew the faith of all on earth,
> The power of salvation streaming thence;
> But as he looks, he feels his very soul
> Pervaded by a new and unknown sense:
> Who added to the cross the wreath of roses?
> It is entwined by blooming, clusters dense,
> Profusely spreading just as though they could
> Endow with softness e'en the rigid wood.
>
> While light and silv'ry clouds, around it soaring,
> Seem heavenward with cross and roses flowing,
> And from the midst like living waters streaming
> A threefold ray from out one core is glowing;
> But not a word surrounds the holy token,
> The meaning of the symbol clearly showing.
> And while the dusk is gath'ring grey and greyer,
> He stands and ponders and is lost in prayer.

27. It is esoterically known that highly-advanced initiates, such as Christian Rosenkreutz, have acquired extraordinary powers and abilities: such as levitation, bi-location, mental telepathy, psychokinesis, astral-travelling, and future-prediction. Also noteworthy, in the case of Master CRC, is the esoteric fact that he has been in continual physical incarnation since the founding of the Rosicrucian Fraternity in the mid-fourteenth century. As confirmed by Rudolf Steiner in a lecture given on

22 May 1907 entitled "The New Form of Wisdom":

> [T]he sources of Rosicrucian wisdom, and above all its great founder, who since its inception had been constantly on the physical plane ... (Published in *Rosicrucian Wisdom: An Introduction*; 2000)

28. This quotation was found in *Rudolf Steiner: A Documentary Biography* by Johannes Hemleben (1975)

29. The following is just a partial list of publications that demonstrate Rudolf Steiner's extensive wealth of Rosicrucian wisdom:

    (1) *Rosicrucianism Renewed* (SteinerBooks; 2007)
    (2) *Rosicrucianism and Modern Initiation* (Rudolf Steiner Press; 2000)
    (3) *Rosicrucian Occult Training* (Kessinger Publishing, LLC; 2010)
    (4) *The Secret Stream: Christian Rosenkreutz and Rosicrucianism* (SteinerBooks; 2000)
    (5) *Rosicrucian Christianity* (Mercury Press; 1989)
    (6) *Rosicrucian Wisdom: An Introduction* (Rudolf Steiner Press; 2000)

CHAPTER 2

30. "Bodhisattva" is a Sanskrit term used to describe a highly-advanced individual who has risen to the level of development where it is no longer necessary to physically incarnate. Nevertheless, they continue to seek rebirth for the benefit of humanity, and not for their own well-being.

    There are various levels of bodhisattva development: some are high initiates, some have advanced to the operating level of an angel, and some have progressed to the sublime level of an archangel.

    The twelve most highly-advanced bodhisattvas are

esoterically known as the "Council of Twelve," the "Mother Lodge of the World," the "Great White Brotherhood" or "The Masters of Wisdom and of the Harmony of Feelings"; and serve the earthly mission of Christ-Jesus from their centre of activity in the etheric realm of Shambhala.

When a bodhisattva decides to no longer physically incarnate, but to serve humanity entirely from the superphysical realms, then they advance to the level of a buddha. The last bodhisattva to become a buddha was Siddhartha Gautama. The next bodhisattva who has decided to become a buddha in the distant future is Lord Maitreya.

31. An "avatar" is a being more advanced than humans (such as an angel or archangel), who freely chooses to incarnate in human form for the sole benefit of mankind. The regent of the sun—the Solar-Christos—who continues to indwell the man Jesus, is the foremost avatar in human history.

32. In a lecture given on 25 February 1909, entitled "Christianity in Human Evolution: Leading Individualities and Avatar Beings," Rudolf Steiner stated the following:

> [T]hese people of the Middle Ages ... was woven into their souls from the astral body of Jesus of Nazareth contained more of what we call the sentient soul, more of the intellectual soul or more of the consciousness soul. This distinction is important because, as you know, the astral body must be envisioned as containing, in a certain sense, all of these three components, as well as the ego, which it encompasses. (Published in *The Principle of Spiritual Economy*, 1986)

33. Esotericists recognize Lucifer as a powerful celestial being who is stubbornly opposed to the divinely-directed

destiny for humanity on earth. Since Lucifer has fallen from his previous high estate due to rebellion against God, he longs to return to his prior glory in the past. Consequently, Lucifer is constantly diverting humanity's attention from the progressive present to the regressive past.

In addition, Lucifer strives to exaggerate, inflame, distort and overly-magnify astral emotions in an attempt to overheat the blood; and thereby distend the ego-forces beyond their proper physical boundaries. This results in an unhealthy decrease in the ethical activity of the ego; which inevitably leads to poor moral judgement.

34. For a much more thorough and detailed analysis and critique of Prokofieff's erroneous anthroposophical ideas, the interested reader is referred to an excellent book by Irina Gordienko (1964–1999) entitled *Sergei O. Prokofieff: Myth and Reality* (2001).

CHAPTER 3

35. As stated by Rudolf Steiner in a lecture given in 18 July 1924:

> [I]n the School of Chartres in the twelfth century, above all by Bernardus Sylvestris and Alanus ab Insulis ... these men did not teach in the Aristotelian way, they did not teach by way of the intellect. They gave their teachings entirely in the form of mighty, imaginative pictures—pictures whereby the spiritual content of Christianity became concretely real. (Published in *Karmic Relationships: Esoteric Studies Vol. VI*; 1989)

36. Scholasticism was a system of philosophical inquiry that was developed in Christian monastic orders during the

Middle Ages. Scholasticism was characterized by an emphasis on dialectical reasoning, rigorous conceptual analysis and the careful formulation of distinctions. The spread of scholasticism throughout Europe resulted in the establishment of the earliest universities.

37. As humorously described by G.K. Chesterton in *St. Thomas Aquinas* (2019):

> [T]here was in Plato a sort of idea that people would be better without their bodies; that their heads might fly off and meet in the sky in merely intellectual marriage, like cherubs in a picture.

38. In a lecture presented on 19 July 1924, Rudolf Steiner stated the following:

> [A]t the beginning of the nineteenth century, to a great, far-reaching Act [of St. Michael] in the spiritual world where that which later on was to become Anthroposophy on the earth was cast into mighty Imaginations [supersensible images]. In the first half of the nineteenth century, and even for a short period at the end of the eighteenth, those who had been Platonists under the teachers of Chartres, who were now living between death and rebirth, and those who had established Aristotelianism on Earth and who had long ago passed through the gate of death—all of them were united in the heavenly realms in a great super-earthly Cult or Ritual. Through this Act all that in the twentieth century was to be spiritually established as the new Christianity after the beginning of the new Michael Age in the last third of the nineteenth century—all this was cast into mighty Imaginations. (Published in *Karmic Relationships: Esoteric Studies Vol. VI*; 1989)

39. The two most influential anthroposophists who have

spread and popularized the fabricated notion that anthroposophy is a modern-day Mystery-religion are Rudolf Grosse (1905–1994) and Sergei O. Prokofieff (1954–2014).

In Grosse's book, *The Christmas Foundation; Beginning of a New Cosmic Age* (1984), he makes the following fallacious statements:

- at the Mystery site of the 20th century, the Dornach Hill.
- a spiritual response to the Goetheanum as a Mystery Centre
- this new social creation, this spirit would be the Spirit of the Goetheanum, the Spirit of the new Mysteries
- its significance for the future of the Goetheanum as a new Mystery Centre
- Rudolf Steiner … brought the stream of the Michael Mysteries down to earth

In Prokofieff's book, *Rudolf Steiner and the Founding of the New Mysteries* (1994), he makes the following fallacious statements:

- The Christmas Conference is a Mystery-event. It is the beginning of the New Mysteries, the Michael Mysteries of esoteric Christianity
- Rudolf Steiner … made for the sake of the founding of the Centre of the New Mysteries, whose central point the Goetheanum was now to become
- the new path of initiation, the path of the New Mysteries whose meaning and content were revealed by Rudolf Steiner only ten years later at the Christmas Conference of 1923-24.
- the foundation of the Goetheanum building, the future centre of the new Christian Mysteries that was to come under the guidance of the Time-Spirit

[Michael] himself

- This is the beginning of the new Michaelic Christianity ... the cosmic Mystery of Michael itself was also unveiled by Rudolf Steiner

40. Anthroposophy is sponsored and inspired by the bodhisattvas of the West—Christian Rosenkreutz and Master Zarathas. As such, it is affiliated with the Rosicrucian Fraternity under the direction of St. Michael the Archangel. Even though the Theosophical Society was the first esoteric public society in history, it was unfortunately corrupted by nefarious Eastern initiates and highjacked to India, primarily for partisan political reasons.

41. The Catholic Rosary arranges the twenty identified Christ-mysteries into four groups of five, as follows:

1. The Joyful Mysteries:
   - The Annunciation
   - The Visitation
   - The Nativity
   - The Presentation of Jesus at the Temple
   - The Finding of Jesus in the Temple

2. The Sorrowful Mysteries:
   - The Agony in the Garden
   - The Scourging at the Pillar
   - The Crowning with Thorns
   - The Carrying of the Cross
   - The Crucifixion and Death of our Lord

3. The Glorious Mysteries:
   - The Resurrection
   - The Ascension
   - The Descent of the Holy Spirit
   - The Assumption of Mary
   - The Coronation of the Virgin

4. The Luminous Mysteries:
   - The Baptism of Jesus in the Jordan
   - The Wedding at Cana
   - Jesus' Proclamation of the Kingdom of God
   - The Transfiguration
   - The Institution of the Eucharist

42. This profound evolutionary transformation was succinctly stated by Steiner as follows:

> [T]he ancient [Mystery] wisdom will reappear in the [spiritual] science of modern times. (From a lecture given on 25 October 1906 entitled "The Occult Significance of Blood: An Esoteric Study")

43. One example of this less-confusing language was expressed by Rudolf Steiner in connection with Class Lesson 9 given on 22 April 1924:

> It goes without saying that everything achieved through esoteric work up to this point flows into the work of the School. For the School is the esoteric foundation and source of all esoteric work within the Anthroposophical Movement.

44. Lucifer's tragic longing was described by Rudolf Steiner in a lecture given on 21 August 1911 entitled "Wonders of the World":

> Lucifer himself takes part in Earth evolution with the perpetual longing within him for his true home, for the star Venus outside in the cosmos. That is the salient feature of the Luciferic nature seen from the cosmic aspect. Clairvoyant consciousness comes to know just what the star of Venus is by entering into the soul of Lucifer, thus experiencing from the Earth Lucifer's tragic longing, like a wonderful cosmic nostalgia, for the star Phosphorus, Lucifer or Venus.

45. Regarding the School of Spiritual Science., Rudolf Steiner made some conflicting remarks, specifically about the First Class. In some instances he indicated that the nineteen lessons were to be followed by two more sections in the First Class. In other instances, he indicated that the First Class had no other content other than the nineteen lessons; such as his concluding remarks given at Class Lesson 19 on 02 August 1924:

> With this, my dear brothers and sisters, in a sense we have completed the First Class of the School. We have allowed the communications that we can receive from the spiritual worlds to pass before our souls, for this is a school established by the spiritual world itself.

46. In his recorded lectures and books, Rudolf Steiner repeatedly emphasized that there were two very effective paths of initiation appropriate to the modern Christian age: (1) the path of Mystic-Christianity, and (2) the path of Rosicrucian-Christianity. As such, there was no esoteric need for a third initiatory path.

47. *Following Christ Across the Threshold: The Non-Initiate's Guide to Entering the Spiritual World* (2019) can be purchased from Amazon. com.

48. Two such examples of diabolical attack on the Anthroposophical Society were the arson-induced destruction of the House of St. John (the Johannesbau) on New Year's Eve, 1922; and the non-fatal poisoning of Rudolf Steiner on New Year's Day, 1923.

49. The General Anthroposophical Society expulsions that unfortunately occurred in 1935 (to which Marie Steiner in 1948 admitted were a mistake) were no doubt demonically incited by the forces of Sorath; who had begun to rise up out of the abyss in 1933. These same diabolical forces were also propelling Nazism to power in Germany during this period.

50. In a similar manner to when Christ-Jesus biblically declared—

> And I say also unto thee, That thou art Peter, and upon this rock I will build my church; and the gates of hell shall not prevail against it. (Matt 16:18)—

the Christ-inspired forces of St. Michael, were not about to let the "gates of hell" prevail against the Anthroposophical Society as well.

CHAPTER 4

51. In his book, *The Philosophy of Spiritual Activity* (1986), Rudolf Steiner declared:

> [T]he first part, which presents intuitive thinking as an inward spiritual activity ...

> The argument of this book is built up on the fact of intuitive thinking, which may be experienced in a purely spiritual way ... ("Ultimate Questions: The Consequences of Monism")

52. Rudolf Steiner, in a lecture from 20 September 1924, spoke of a "Beast" that would rise up in 1933. This is a reference to the "two-horned Beast [Sorath] that rises from the bottomless pit" in St. John's book of Revelation:

> In 1933, dear friends, there would be a possibility for the earth and everything living on it to perish if there did not exist also that other wise arrangement that cannot be calculated ... Before the Etheric Christ can be comprehended by human beings in the right way, humanity must first cope with encountering the Beast who will rise up in 1933. (Published in *The Book of Revelation and the Work of the Priest*; 1999)

53. Even though the triad of evil didn't become an identifiable inimical alliance until Sorath began to rise up out of the abyss in 1933, certain statements made by Rudolf Steiner indicate that he anticipated its future formation; as in the following:

> We can understand the world in the right way only when we see it based on this triad and are perfectly clear that human life is the beam of the scales. Here is the fulcrum: on one side is the Luciferic element, actually pulling the pan upward; opposite is the Ahrimanic element, pushing the pan downward. Our human task—our human essence—is to keep the beam balanced.
>
> Now, as you may well imagine, it lies in the deepest interests of the Luciferic and Ahrimanic powers to conceal this secret of the number three—after all, the proper penetration of this secret would allow humanity to bring about the state of balance between the Luciferic and Ahrimanic powers. (From a lecture given on 21 November 1919, and published in *The Archangel Michael: His Mission and Ours*; 1994)

54. Esoterically, the Holy Spirit is better known as the "Holy Mother-Spirit" or the "Holy Mother" since she is the divine personification of the feminine nature of God; which is the omniscient wisdom that expands outwardly into infinity.

   For a much more detailed explanation, the interested reader is referred to this author's previous publication, *The Greater Mysteries of the Divine Trinity, the Logos-Word and Creation* (2015); available from Amazon.com.

55. In a lecture given on 25 August 1913, Rudolf Steiner echoed the necessary polar-balancing of Lucifer and Ahriman as follows:

These beings we call Ahriman and Lucifer are right here in the world, they have their task in the universal order, and one cannot sweep them away. Besides, it is not a question of annihilating them, but—as in the case of the weights on both sides of the scales—the ahrimanic and luciferic forces must balance each other in their influence on human beings and on other beings. (Published in *Secrets of the Threshold*, 1987)

56. For those unfamiliar with Steiner's well-known wooden sculpture, the central figure depicts the Christ-being who stands between Lucifer and Ahriman. Lucifer is depicted in a carved celestial region in the top-left corner above Christ as a sad angel-face with broken wings. Ahriman is depicted in a subterranean cave below Christ as an agonized figure entangled in vines.

57. For far greater detail and explanation of Christ-Jesus and the inverse triad of evil, the interested reader is referred to this author's previous publication, *From Darkness to Light: Divine Love and the Transmutation of Evil* (2016); available from Amazon.com.

58. Some esotericists have mistakenly speculated that Sorath is the destined Antichrist, on the basis that his evil intention is to illicitly usurp the rightful leadership of the Solar-Christos (the Christ-Being) and unlawfully control the entire solar system. For this reason, Sorath has been esoterically known as the "Sun-Demon." Furthermore, since Sorath is known to be an ancient evil-entity from a degenerate evolution alien to our own, he has no karmically-determined physical incarnation within the rightful stream of earth evolution.

59. As stated by Rudolf Steiner in a lecture given on 01 November 1919:

[B]efore only a part of the third millennium of the post-Christian era has elapsed, there will be, in the

West, an actual incarnation of Ahriman: Ahriman in the flesh. Humanity on earth cannot escape this incarnation of Ahriman. It will come inevitably. But what matters is that people shall find the right vantage point from which to confront it. (Published in *The Incarnation of Ahriman: The Embodiment of Evil on Earth*; 2006)

60. Rudolf Steiner revealed this information in a lecture given on 15 November 1919:

> As soon as Ahriman incarnates at the destined time in the West, the whole of culture would be impregnated with his forces ... Through certain stupendous acts he would bring to humanity all the clairvoyant knowledge which until then can be acquired only by dint of intense labor and effort. People could live on as materialists ... When Ahriman incarnates in the West at the appointed time, he would establish a great occult school for the practice of magic arts of the greatest grandeur, and what otherwise can be acquired only by strenuous effort would be poured over humankind. (Published in *The Influences of Lucifer and Ahriman;* 1993)

61. During his years as a community organizer in Chicago, Barak Obama became a student and supporter of radical-socialist, Saul Alinski (1909–1972) who wrote the infamous *Rules for Radicals: A Pragmatic Primer for Realistic Radicals* (2010). During that time, Obama completed the national training course taught by the Industrial Areas Foundation, the community organizing school founded by Alinsky. Obama later went on to teach Alinsky's radical-socialist concepts and methods at community organizing workshops and seminars in Southside Chicago.

62. When Obama traveled to China in 2009, radical-socialist,

multi-billionaire funder—George Soros—was asked:

> What sort of financial deal should Obama be seeking to strike when he travels to China next month?

Soros replied:

> No, I think this would be the time because you really need to bring China into the creation of a New World Order.

When subsequently asked:

> Is there going to be some tipping point, a moment at which the [US] dollar is fatally weakened, or does it just sort of carry on?

To which Soros replied:

> An orderly decline of the dollar is actually desirable. A decline in the value of the dollar is necessary in order to compensate for the fact that the US economy will remain rather weak; will be a drag on the global economy. China will emerge as the motor replacing the US consumer ... China will be the engine driving it forward, and the US will be actually a drag that's being pulled along through a gradual decline in the value of the dollar ...

63. There is a Catholic tradition depicted in numerous statues of Blessed Mary that shows her foot immobilizing the head of a serpent. Esoterically understood, the wisdom of the Holy Mother Spirit that infuses the soul of Blessed Mary is able to paralyze the materialistic thought of the Ahrimanic dragon.

CONCLUSION

64. This is a phrase from the Catholic "Prayer to St. Michael the Archangel," which has become re-popularized during these dark spiritual times. It reads as follows:

> St. Michael the Archangel, defend us in battle.
> Be our defense against the wickedness
> and snares of the Devil.
> May God rebuke him, we humbly pray;
> and do thou, O Prince of the heavenly hosts,
> by the power of God, thrust into hell Satan,
> and all the evil spirits, who prowl about the world
> seeking the ruin of souls.
> Amen.

SELECT BIBLIOGRAPHY

(in alphabetical order)

- Andrew George (translator), *The Epic of Gilgamesh* (Penguin Classics, 2003)

- *Catechism of the Catholic Church* (Libreria Editrice Vaticana, 2000)

- *Compendium: Catechism of the Catholic Church* (USCCB, 2006)

- Fulton J. Sheen, *Communism and the Conscience of the West* (Refuge of Sinners Publishing, Inc., 1948)

- G.K. Chesterton, *St. Thomas Aquinas* (Dover Publications, Inc., 2019)

- Irina Gordienko, *Sergei O. Prokofieff: Myth and Reality* (Lochmann-Verlag, 2001)

- Johannes Hemleben, *Rudolf Steiner: A Documentary Biography* (Henry Goulden Limited, 1975)

- Johann Wolfgang von Goethe, *The Mysteries, A Poem by Goethe and a Lecture by Rudolf Steiner* (Mercury Press, 1987)

- Johann Wolfgang von Goethe, *The Fairy Tale of the Green Snake and the Beautiful Lily* (Floris Books, 1979)

- Ken Wilber, *The Marriage of Sense and Soul: Integrating Science and Religion* (Harmony, 1999)

- Ron MacFarlane, *Following Christ Across the Threshold: The Non-Initiate's Guide to Entering the Spiritual World* (Greater Mysteries Publications, 2019)

- Ron MacFarlane, *From Darkness to Light: Divine Love and the Transmutation of Evil* (Greater Mysteries Publications, 2016)

- Ron MacFarlane, *The Greater Mysteries of the Divine Trinity, the Logos-Word and Creation* (Greater Mysteries Publications, 2015)

- RSV-CE, *The Bible* (Ignatius Press, 1966)

- Rudolf Grosse, *The Christmas Foundation; Beginning of a New Cosmic Age* (SteinerBooks, 1984)

- Rudolf Steiner, *Anthroposophical Leading Thoughts* (Rudolf Steiner Press, 1973)

- Rudolf Steiner, *Anthroposophy and Christianity* (Anthroposophic Press, 1985)

- Rudolf Steiner, *Christ in Relation to Lucifer and Ahriman* (Anthroposophic Press, 1978)

- Rudolf Steiner, *Karmic Relationships: Esoteric Studies Vol. III* (Rudolf Steiner Press, 2009)

- Rudolf Steiner, *Karmic Relationships: Esoteric Studies Vol. VI* (Rudolf Steiner Press, 1989)

- Rudolf Steiner, *Rosicrucian Wisdom: An Introduction* (Rudolf Steiner Press, 2000)

- Rudolf Steiner, *Secrets of the Threshold* (The Anthroposophic Press, 1987)

- Rudolf Steiner, *The Archangel Michael: His Mission and Ours* (SteinerBooks, 1994)

- Rudolf Steiner, *The Book of Revelation and the Work of the Priest* (Rudolf Steiner Press, 1999)

- Rudolf Steiner, *The Course of My Life* (Rudolf Steiner Press, 1986)

- Rudolf Steiner, *The Incarnation of Ahriman: The Embodiment of Evil on Earth* (Rudolf Steiner Press, 2006)

- Rudolf Steiner, *The Influences of Lucifer and Ahriman* (The Anthroposophic Press, 1993)

- Rudolf Steiner, *The Philosophy of Spiritual Activity* (Anthroposophic Press, 1986)

- Rudolf Steiner, *The Principle of Spiritual Economy* (SteinerBooks, 1986)

- Saint Augustine, *Confessions* (Hackett Publishing Company, Inc., 2006)

- Saul Alinski, *Rules for Radicals: A Pragmatic Primer for Realistic Radicals* (Vintage Books, 2010)

- Sergei O. Prokofieff, *Rudolf Steiner and the Founding of the New Mysteries* (Temple Lodge Publishing, 1994)

- T.H. Meyer (editor), *The First Class Lessons and Mantras: The Michael School Meditative Path in Nineteen Steps* (SteinerBooks, 2016)

- Thomas J. McFarlane, *Sacred Science: Essays on Mathematics, Physics and Spiritual Philosophy* (www.integralscience.org, 1995)

OTHER BOOKS BY

RON MACFARLANE

THERE IS a puzzling and pervasive misconception in present-day thinking that the existence of God cannot be intellectually determined, and that mentally accepting the existence of God is strictly a matter of non-rational belief (faith).

As such, contemplating God's existence is erroneously regarded as the exclusive subject of faith-based or speculative ideologies (religion and philosophy) which have no proper place in natural scientific study.

The fact is, there are a number of very convincing intellectual arguments concerning the existence of God that have been around for hundreds of years. Indeed, the existence of God can be determined with compelling intellectual certainty—provided the thinker honestly wishes to do so. Moreover, recent advances and discoveries in science have not weakened previous intellectual arguments for God's existence, but instead have enormously strengthened and supported them.

Intellectually assenting to the existence of God is easily demonstrated to be a superlatively logical conclusion, not some vague irrational conceptualization. Remarkably, at the present time there are only two seriously-competing intellectual explanations of life: the existence of God (the "God-hypothesis") and the existence of infinite universes (the "multiverse theory"). The postulation of an infinite number of unobservable universes is clearly a desperate attempt by atheistic scientists to avoid the God-hypothesis as the most credible and logical intellectual explanation of life and the universe. Moreover, under intellectual scrutiny, the scientifically celebrated "evolutionary theory" is here demonstrated to be fatally-flawed (philosophically illogical) as a credible explanation of life.

In this particular discourse, five well-known intellectual arguments for God's existence will be thoroughly examined. In considering these arguments, every attempt has been made to include current contributions, advances and discoveries that have modernized the more traditional arguments. Prior to examining these particular arguments for God, the universal predilection to establish intellectual 'oneness'—"monism"—will be considered in detail as well as the recurring propensity to postulate the existence of one supreme being—"monotheism."

Once intellectual certainty of one Supreme Being is established, a number of divine attributes can be logically deduced as well. Eleven of these attributes will be determined and examined in greater detail.

This book is available to order from Amazon.com

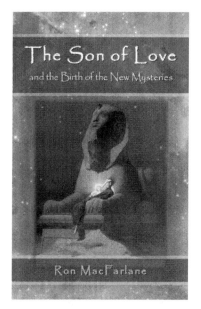

The Son of Love
and the Birth of the New Mysteries

Ron MacFarlane

FOR COUNTLESS esoteric students today, the Mystery centres of ancient times have retained a powerful and fascinating allure. Moreover, there is often a wishful longing to revive and continue their secretive initiatory activity into modern times.

Unfortunately, this anachronistic longing is largely based on an illusionary misunderstanding of these Mysteries and the real reasons for their destined demise.

The primary reason for the disappearance of the ancient Mysteries is that they have been supplanted by the superior new mysteries—the mysteries of the Son. These new mysteries were initiated by Christ-Jesus himself. In order to better understand these Son-mysteries in a spiritually-scientific way, Rudolf Steiner (1861–1925) established the Anthroposophical Movement and Society.

Unfortunately, anthroposophy today has become unduly influenced by members and leaders who long to transform spiritual science into a modern-day Mystery institution. Moreover, contrary to his own words and intentions, Rudolf Steiner is even claimed to be the founder of some new "Michael-Mysteries."

By carefully establishing a correct esoteric understanding of the ancient pagan Mysteries, as well as a better appreciation of the new mysteries of the Son, this well-researched and readable discourse convincingly shows that all current and past attempts to revive the ancient pagan Mysteries regressively diverts human development backward to the seducer of mankind, Lucifer, rather than progressively forward to the saviour of mankind, Christ-Jesus.

Moreover, by additionally tracing the intriguing historical

development of esoteric Christianity (particularly the Knights of the Holy Grail and Rosicrucianism) alongside Freemasonry, the Knights Templar and Theosophy, this important and necessary study illuminates the correct esoteric position and true significance of anthroposophical spiritual science.

This book is available to order from Amazon.com

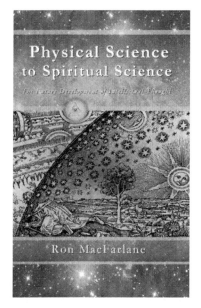

THE PRIDE OF civilized mankind—intellectual thinking—is at a critical crossroads today. No doubt surprising to many, the cognitive capacity to consciously formulate abstract ideas in the mind, and then to manipulate them according to devised rules of logic in order to acquire new knowledge has only been humanly possible for about the last 3,000 years. Prior to intellectual (abstract) thinking, mental activity characteristically consisted of vivid pictorial images that arose spontaneously in the human mind from natural and supernatural stimuli.

The ability to think abstractly is the necessary foundation for mathematics, language and empirical science. The developmental history of intellectual thought, then, exactly parallels the developmental history of mathematics, language and science. Moreover, since abstract thinking inherently encourages the cognitive separation of subject (the thinker) and object (the perceived environment), the history of intellectual development also parallels the historical development of self-conscious (ego) awareness.

Over the last 3000 years, mankind in general has slowly perfected intellectual thinking; and thereby developed complex mathematics, sophisticated languages, comprehensively-detailed empirical sciences and pronounced ego-awareness. Unfortunately, all this intellectual activity over the many previous centuries has also exclusively strengthened human awareness of the physical, material world and substantially decreased awareness of the superphysical spiritual world.

That is why today, intellectual thinking is at a critical crossroads in further development. Thinking (intellectual or otherwise) is a superphysical activity—an activity within the soul. Empirical science is incorrect in postulating that physical brain tissue generates thought. The brain is simply the biological "sending and receiving" apparatus: sending sense-perceptions to the soul and receiving thought-conceptions from the soul. All this activity certainly generates chemical and electrical activity within the brain; but this activity is the effect, not the cause of thinking.

The danger to future intellectual thought is that increased acceptance of the erroneous scientific notion that thinking is simply brain-chemistry will increasingly deny and deaden true superphysical thinking. Future thinking runs the risk of becoming "a self-fulfilled prophecy"—the more people fervently believe that thought is simply brain-chemistry, the more thought will indeed become simply brain-chemistry. As a result, future human beings will be less responsible for generating their own thinking activity and more involuntarily controlled by their own brain chemistry. The artificial intelligence of machines won't become more human; but instead human beings will become more like robotic machines.

Presently, then, empirical science is leading intellectual thinking in a downward, materialistic direction. Correspondingly, however, true spiritual science (anthroposophy) is also actively engaged in leading intellectual thought back to its superphysical source in the soul. *Physical Science to Spiritual Science: the Future Development of Intellectual Thought* begins by examining the historical development of intellectual thinking and the corresponding rise of physical science. Once this has been discussed, practical and detailed information is presented on how spiritual science is leading intellectual thinking back to its true soul-source. It is intended that upon completion of this discourse, sincere and open-minded readers will themselves come to experience the exhilarating, superphysical nature of their own intellectual thought.

This book is available to order from Amazon.com

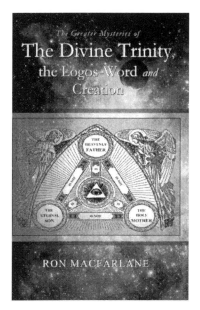

THE DIVINE TRINITY—the greatest of all Christian mysteries. How is it that the one God is a unity of three divine persons? Christ-Jesus first revealed this mystery to his disciples when on earth. Later, around the sixth century, the Trinitarian mystery was theologically clarified and outlined by the formulation of the Athanasian Creed. Conceptual understanding of the divine Trinity has changed very little in Western society since then. Similarly with the theological understanding of the Logos-Word, as mentioned in the Gospel of St. John. The traditional understanding, that has remained essentially unchallenged for centuries, is that the Logos-Word is synonymous with God the Son. As for creation, the best that mainstream Christianity has historically provided is an ancient, allegorical account contained in the Book of Genesis.

Out of the hidden well-springs of esoteric Christianity, and as the title indicates, *The Greater Mysteries of the Divine Trinity, the Logos-Word and Creation*, delves much more deeply into the profound mysteries of the Trinitarian God, the Logos-Word of St. John and the creation of the universe. The divine Trinity is here demonstrated to be the loving union of Heavenly Father, Holy Mother and Eternal Son. The Logos-Word is here evidenced to be the "Universal Man," the primordial cosmic creation of God the Son. Universal creation itself is here detailed to be the "one life becoming many"—the multiplication of the Logos-Word into countless individualized life-forms and beings.

The depth and breadth of original and thought-provoking information presented here will, no doubt, stimulate and excite those esoteric thinkers who are seriously seeking answers to the deeper mysteries of life, existence and the universe.

This book is available to order from Amazon.com

Ron MacFarlane

The Star of Higher Knowledge

The Five Guiding Mysteries of Esoteric Christianity

WHEN CHRIST-JESUS walked the earth over two thousand years ago, he established a two-fold division in his teaching that has continued to this day. To the general public, he simplified his teaching and presented it in pictorial, allegorical and figurative imagery in the form of stories, parables and lessons that could be imaginatively and intuitively understood.

To his inner circle of disciples (who were sufficiently prepared), however, he taught intellectual concepts, clear ideas and logical reasoning that could be understood on a much deeper and wider level of comprehension. As biblically explained:

> Then the disciples came and said to him, "Why do you speak to them [the general public] in parables?" And he answered them, "To you it has been given to know the secrets of the kingdom of heaven, but to them it has not been given ... This is why I speak to them in parables, because seeing they do not see, and hearing they do not hear, nor do they understand." (Matt 13:10, 13)

Moreover, in union with the divine, Our Saviour was able to reveal sacred knowledge that had never been previously presented in the entire history of mankind: "I will explain mysteries hidden since the creation of the world" (Matt 13:35). This sacred and revealed knowledge has been termed "Christ-mysteries" or "mysteries of the Son."

After his glorious resurrection and ascension, Christ-Jesus institutionalized his two-fold mystery-teachings through St. Peter and St. John (the evangelist, not the apostle). Through St. Peter, Our Saviour instituted a universal Christian *religion* and *theology* to preserve, promote and convey the more basic and simplified mystery-teachings that are intended for the general public. Through St. John, Christ-Jesus instituted a universal Christian *philosophy* and *theosophy* to preserve, promote and convey the more comprehensive and complex mystery-teachings that are intended for the more advanced disciples (Christian initiates). In esoteric terminology, the institutionalized teachings through St. Peter are known as the "lesser mysteries of exoteric Christianity." The institutionalized teachings through St. John are known as the "greater mysteries of esoteric Christianity."

While both mystery-teaching approaches are equally sacred, profound and intended to complement each other, corrupt and intolerant authorities within the universal institution (Church) of St. Peter, for many centuries, persecuted and attacked any public expressions of esoteric Christianity. Consequently, genuine historical forms of esoteric Christianity, such as the Knights of the Holy Grail and the Fraternity of the Rose-Cross, were forced to be secretive and publically-hidden during the past two thousand years.

Thankfully today, the social, political and intellectual climate has progressed to the point where the greater mystery-teachings of esoteric Christianity can begin to be publically revealed for the first time. This modern-day outpouring really began with the twentieth-century establishment of anthroposophy by Rudolf Steiner (1861–1925). The information and approach presented in *The Star of Higher Knowledge: The Five Guiding Mysteries of Esoteric Christianity* is intended to augment and continue the mystery-teachings of Christ-Jesus as safeguarded by the Rosicrucian Fraternity and publicized through anthroposophy.

Consequently, this particular discourse delves much more deeply and comprehensively into the cosmos-changing salvational achievement of Christ-Jesus: the historical and cosmic preparations; as well as his birth, life, death, resurrection and ascension. While much of this mystery information may be unfamiliar, unknown and unexpected to mainstream (exoteric) Christianity, it in no way is meant to criticize, denigrate or displace the profound teachings of the universal Church; but rather, to complement, to enhance and to enlarge—for the betterment of true Christianity and, thereby, the betterment of all mankind.

This book is available to order from Amazon.com

Also check out the authour's website:

www.heartofshambhala.com

A Site Dedicated to True Esoteric Christianity

Contemporary Christianity, the world religion established by the God-Man, Christ-Jesus, and founded on the revelatory-principle that "God is love," is hardly the shining example of ideological unity and universal brotherhood that it was intended to be. There are approximately 41,000 different Christian denominations in the world today, many of which are fervently hostile to each other.

Atheistic and anti-Christian polemicists have concluded that there is something inherently wrong with Christianity itself and, in consequence, it is doomed to failure and eventual extinction.

Discerning Christian advocates, however, know that any apparent failure to realize the high ideals of Christianity is not due to the profound teachings and the illustrious life-example of Christ-Jesus, but instead to the limitations of wounded human nature. Corrupt, power-hungry, destructive and evil-minded human beings have twisted, distorted and fragmented true Christianity for the past two thousand years, and continue to do so today.

Moreover, on a much deeper spiritual level, since Christianity is indeed a divinely-initiated endeavor to help restore "fallen" humanity, powerful and demonic beings have attempted to destroy nascent Christianity from its very inception. But thankfully, according to Christ-Jesus himself, "the powers of hell will not prevail against it [Christianity]" (Matt 16:18).

Sadly contributing to the injurious fragmentation of Christianity—the "religion of divine love"—is the sectarian hostility between certain proponents of anthroposophy and select members of the Catholic Church. In both cases, this is largely due to ignorance; that is, an almost complete lack of understanding about the true significance and mission of the other—anthroposophical critics know almost nothing of Catholicism, and Catholic critics know almost nothing about anthroposophy.

The wonderful reconciliatory fact is that anthroposophy and Catholicism are not conflicting polar opposites, but are instead like two sides of the same golden coin—different, but complementary. Instead of only one side or the other being the only true approach to Christ-Jesus, both are uniquely necessary and both positively contribute to the complete truth of Christianity.

Since this author is happily and harmoniously both an anthroposophist and a Catholic, *The Greater and Lesser Mysteries of Christianity: The Complementary Paths of Anthroposophy and Catholicism* earnestly seeks to correct the misinformation and lack of understanding that each partisan critic has for the other. As in almost every significant dispute, increased knowledge and familiarity about each other will in time bring both sides closer together for mutual growth and benefit.

This book is available to order from Amazon.com

IN THE LIGHT of spiritual science, never before in the history of the world has there been such an assailment of supernatural evil upon humanity as extensive and intense as there exists at the present time. Subconsciously pouring into the human soul are the seductive whisperings of Luciferic beings and fallen angels; the perceptual distortions of Ahrimanic (Satanic) beings; the lurid, egocentric promptings of corrupt spirits of personality (asuras); and the violent inducements of blood-lust rising up from the subterranean "beast of Revelation" (Sorath the sun-demon).

The tragic and bitter irony of all this, however, is that because of today's pervasive, atheistic and secular culture and the materialistic worldview of natural science, individual human beings are correspondingly the most oblivious to supernatural evil than they have ever been at any other time in world history.

To be sure, people today are certainly aware of the *effects* of supernatural evil—extensive and increased natural disasters; horrific instances of mass genocide; the prolific use of torture and brutality by government agencies; individual acts of sudden cruelty and murder; pathological selfishness throughout the world's business and financial markets; strange, globally-infectious viral contagions; the devaluation of human life through abortion and euthanasia; and a world-wide pandemic of dehumanizing drug addiction. What most people today fail to realize is that the invisible fomenting agents—the *causes*—of all these life-threatening, destructive physical events and pathologies are ultimately rooted in the impulses of supernatural evil.

To be sure, mankind would have completely and totally succumbed to this tsunami of supernatural evil if it weren't for the protective and opposing intervention of powerful, benevolent celestial beings, such as St. Michael the Archai, Yahweh-Elohim (the spirit of the moon), and the Solar-Christos (aka: "Christ"—the regent of the sun).

More than ever, it is crucially important in today's world to understand the nature of evil, and to become more aware and cognizant of the various perpetrators of supernatural evil. Thereby, conscious cooperation with the compassionate protectors and guardians of mankind can be increased and strengthened, so that supernatural evil is better resisted and eventually overcome.

To this end, *From Darkness to Light: Divine Love and the Transmutation of Evil* delves deeply into the thorny questions of "What exactly is evil?"; together with "How and when did evil begin?"; as well as "Why does God allow evil to exist?" Once the nature, genesis and purpose of evil is better understood, then various influential superphysical perpetrators of supernatural evil will be examined in closer detail. Correspondingly, the superphysical proponents of cosmic holiness will be identified and better understood as well.

Wherever possible, the spiritual-scientific research of anthroposophy—an independent offshoot of the Rosicrucian Fraternity, and the modern-day expression of esoteric Christianity that was established by Rudolf Steiner (1861–1925)—will be included and referenced. Following this profoundly-esoteric background, the destined human struggle with continuing and obdurate evil—far into the future development of the earth—will also be mentally envisioned and supersensibly examined.

It is sincerely intended that upon completion of the entire written discourse, concerned individuals will be better armed and shielded in order to become actively engaged on the side of holiness and spiritual light in the prolonged cosmic battle against evil and material darkness.

NO DOUBT, anyone interested in Christian esotericism will have noticed that there is a widespread modern-day revival of interest in the ancient gnostic concept of "Sophia" amongst a strange diversity of groups: wiccans, neo-pagans, New Agers, neo-gnostics, Catholic mystics, Orthodox Christians, radical feminists and anthropos-ophists. Adding to this ideological mélange is the exotic variety of Sophia designations and conceptions: the Divine Sophia, the heavenly-sophia, the earthly-sophia, Hagia Sophia, the goddess Sophia, the Aeon Sophia, the Virgin Sophia, Sophia-Achamoth, Pistis Sophia, Isis-Sophia, Jesus Sophia, theo-sophia, philo-sophia and anthropo-sophia.

Not surprisingly, then, this cacophony of Sophias is very often contradictory, confusing, distorted, invented, erroneous, and (sadly) rarely enlightening. It is not difficult to detect that "esoteric entrepreneurs" have seized this current "thirst for Sophia" to offer up a potpourri of books, courses, conferences, workshops, lessons, websites, video clips, internet articles—even worship services—to inundate, titillate and financially captivate any novice Sophia seeker.

So, what is a sincere Christian esotericist to make of this fervent Sophia phenomenon: "Is it a positive and healthy spiritual development, or is it a regressive and outmoded religious diversion?" This particular discourse—*Mary and the Divine Sophia*—delves deeply and genuinely into this important question in order to establish spiritual fact from unspiritual fiction.

In order to adequately answer this question, however, profound esoteric investigation into the Trinitarian nature of God, as well as the universal being of the Logos-Word, together with the fundamental underlying principles of the created cosmos will need to be detailed and discussed. Some of this previously-guarded esoteric information may be quite new and unfamiliar to many readers; but every effort has been made to present it in clear, understandable concepts.

Furthermore, since the mother of Jesus is very often intimately associated or connected to historical and present-day conceptions of Sophia, a comprehensive study will also be undertaken regarding Mary and her special relationship to the Divine Sophia; relying heavily on the spiritual-scientific research of Austrian philosopher and esotericist, Rudolf Steiner (1861–1925). Once again, a great deal of this information will be startlingly new to those unfamiliar with anthroposophy; but, as before, great care has been taken to present this possibly-unfamiliar information in a comprehensible, intellectually-accessible way.

It is sincerely intended that this discourse will provide the earnest esotericist with reliable, trustworthy and objective spiritual knowledge in order to confidently know and understand the mystery-truth of the heavenly-sophia; and thereby extricate her from the distortions and falsifications of Lucifer and Ahriman.

This book is available to order from Amazon.com

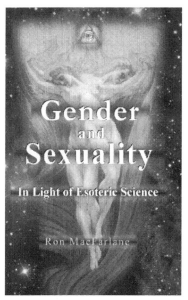

SINCE THE DAWN of mankind, human beings have unquestioningly accepted the self-evident biological truth that there are only two distinct sexes—male and female. Furthermore, this truth was understood to be divinely established, as indicated in the ancient Hebrew writings of Moses: "So God created man in his own image … male and female he created them. And God blessed them" (Gen 1:27, 28).

Similarly with the concomitant truth that there are only two distinct genders—masculine and feminine. Moreover, in ancient times the dual genders were seen as fundamental and complementary universal principles that infused and fashioned everything in the created cosmos. One familiar expression of this ancient metaphysical belief is the Chinese Taoist principles of yin and yang.

Throughout history, stable and productive family units, tribal groupings, social communities, and even vast empires were globally established on the exigent foundational truths of sexuality and gender—that is—until very recently.

Beginning in the mid-1950s, what had been perennially and universally accepted regarding sex and gender began to be academically questioned and challenged. This ideological heterodoxy quickly accelerated in the 1960s with the inception and radical cultural impact of the sexual revolution and the feminist movement. Increased and well-organized gay and lesbian activism in the 1970s also did much to publicly reject the traditional dichotomies of male–female and masculine–feminine in order to promote a novel range of non-normative sexualities and exotic gender categories.

By the early 2000s, sociological theorists, academic institutions, media organizations, civil rights groups, medical associations, political parties, national governments and international agencies were all becoming involved in a cultural drive to "mainstream" this radically-new and socially-transformative gender ideology.

But to a large percentage of today's citizens throughout Western society, this cultural revolution of gender ideology has been unexpectedly and uninvitedly infiltrating their established lives and communities with a discordant cacophony of bizarre sexual and gender ideas, terms and expressions; such as: gender identity, gender expression, gender roles, gender socialization, gender fluidity, gender ambiguity (ambigender), third gender (trigender), non-binary gender, non-gender, gender neutral, agender, gender dysphoria, gender perspective, genderqueer, biological gender, hormonal gender, gonadic gender, cisgender, pangender, transgender, sexual orientation, bisexual, transsexual, intersexual, omnisexual, asexual, androgynous and two-spirit.

While even to casual observation, it is evident that this contemporary sexual revolution is causing fierce political and social upheaval, what can be perplexing to a deeper spiritual analysis are questions such as: "What exactly are sexuality and gender; and are they synonymous or different? What is causing the current sexual revolution? Why is it occurring at this particular time in world history? Is this sexual revolution progressive or regressive; beneficial or harmful? Are there spiritual forces and beings involved in this upheaval; and are they godly or evil?"

Though these questions can certainly be spiritually addressed by traditional Western theology, a much deeper, meaningful, lasting and comprehensive understanding can only be provided by the superphysical research and hidden wisdom of esoteric science.

This particular discourse, then—*Gender and Sexuality in Light of Esoteric Science*—heavily relies on ancient Yogic teachings, age-old Egyptian Hermetic philosophy, hidden Rosicrucian wisdom and the anthroposophical research of clairvoyant investigator, Rudolf Steiner (1861–1925) to profoundly and penetratingly address these important questions.

Esoteric science will convincingly explain why there are, in reality, only two sexes—male and female; and only two genders—masculine and feminine. Anything else is an unreal and delusional abstraction, hypothesis or conjecture.

In order to rationally embrace the binary truth of gender—masculine and feminine—it will be necessary to first understand the Trinitarian nature of God, and then perceive how the divine nature is faithfully reflected throughout the created universe, including human existence. After which, in order to similarly embrace the binary truth of human sexuality—male and female—it will be necessary to clairvoyantly trace the history and development of mankind on earth, back to far-distant primordial ages.

It will be shown that throughout human existence on earth, powerful supernatural beings and forces—both beneficial and inimical—have been intimately and significantly involved in the evolution and development of human sexuality. Moreover, despite the appalling lack of contemporary human awareness, this supernatural involvement has continued into the present day.

The much-celebrated "freedoms" brought about by the sexual revolution will be seen and understood to be an inimical supernatural assault on reason, reality, nature and progressive human evolution, particularly by Luciferic and Ahrimanic beings and forces.[2] The current state of sexual and gender confusion, therefore, is not regarded as a positive development by esoteric science; but rather a seriously-harmful and seductive delusionary entrapment that must be challenged, arrested and positively corrected.

This book is available to order from Amazon.com

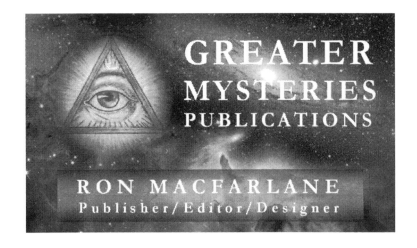

SPIRITUAL WARFARE
IN THE 21ˢᵗ CENTURY
DONALD TRUMP vs THE NEW WORLD ORDER

RON MACFARLANE

A RATHER STRANGE and disturbing social upheaval has been covertly and pervasively occurring throughout the Western world—particularly in America—since the early 1990s. A creeping form of radical-socialism has been gradually infecting Western political parties, academic institutions, medical professions, mainstream news agencies, television and film industries, literary publishing and everyday social interaction for the past three decades.

Perplexingly ironic, as the former Soviet Union and Eastern Bloc States were finally divesting themselves of the failed and oppressive socialist/communist ideology of the past, intellectuals and ideologues throughout the Western world began to eagerly embrace and apply the fundamental tenets of radical-socialism.

This "Westernized" form of socialist ideology is unabashedly atheistic and openly hostile to religion, particularly Christianity, in all its denominational forms. Hypocritically, however, this same "atheistic-socialism" openly supports and defends Muslim believers, who are considered members of a "victimized minority."

The philosophical underpinning of atheistic-socialism is the classic Marxist belief that the social interaction of humanity throughout the ages has entirely and exclusively been a perpetual class struggle between the have-nots and the haves; the poor and the wealthy; the oppressed and the oppressors; the victims and the victimizers. In more Marxist terminology, historical class conflict has been between the "proletariat"—the peasants, labourers and workers; and the "bourgeoisie"—the nobility, landowners, and capitalists.

However, in recent times various activist groups—each one claiming "victimized" status—have adapted basic Marxist ideology to suit their own particular causes and agendas. For example, radical-feminists contend that it is men who are the real historic victimizers and that women are their primary victims. Alternatively, Black, Hispanic and Indigenous activists each claim that they are the continued victims of White, European-based culture. Homosexual activists assert that they are the victims of heterosexual, Judeo-Christian society. All these activists, therefore, blame a common oppressor for their perceived victimized condition—wealthy, White, conservative Christian men.

Moreover, in keeping with classic Marxist ideology, each of these socialist-inspired activist groups fervently believes that the solution to their perceived oppression is not gradual social change and reform; but the revolutionary overthrow of prosperous, White, Christian, male-influenced culture and society.

In essence, then, what is currently taking place throughout Western society is a fierce cultural war being waged by numerous left-leaning activist groups whose primary goal is the destruction of European-based Christian culture. In addition, their ultimate goal is to replace democratic governance through majority rule with an exclusively-atheistic, secular society where political, economic and cultural power is autocratically determined and enforced by centralized State-control that is driven by uncompromising, totalitarian-style minority activism.

In Western nations, this radical atheistic-socialism—recently termed the "alt-left"—has been opportunistically embraced by "left-wing" and "neo-liberal" political parties; but rejected by "right-wing" and "neo-conservative" political parties. Consequently, in America it is the Democratic Party (in general) that espouses and promotes alt-leftist atheistic-socialism; while the Republican Party (in general) rejects and opposes this ideology.

The radical alt-left agenda was enormously accelerated in America during the eight years (2009 to 2017) of Democratic Party

President, Barack Hussein Obama. Primarily through executive order and veto power, Obama enacted and enforced radical-socialist national and international policy on climate change, economic regulation, religion, abortion, de-militarization, same-sex marriage, gun control, immigration, taxation, free-trade and deficit spending.

Moreover, through presidential appointment, Obama politicized and "weaponized" the US intelligence community (FBI, CIA and NSA), the Justice department, the IRS, the Supreme Court and district court systems with radical-socialists and alt-left loyalists. Radical-socialist ideologues within the Democratic Party and their wealthy financial backers (such as George Soros) were totally confident that these "deep-state" operatives in government—together with the predominantly left-leaning communications media in radio, television and newspapers—would guarantee another presidential election victory in 2017.

Moreover, Soros and his billionaire cohorts in the Democratic Alliance had decided that Hillary Rodham Clinton would be the next American president; and had set up a "dirty-tricks" Democratic Party campaign organization (headed by Soros-lackey John Podesta) to further continue and advance their accelerating alt-left cultural revolution.

Despite pre-election propaganda by major leftist-media (such as ABC, CNN, MSNBC, the NY Times and Washington Post) that Hillary Clinton would win the presidential election by a "landslide victory"; despite the DNC (Democratic National Committee) and the Clinton election organizers conducting a corrupt, "shady-tactics" campaign in order to guarantee victory; and despite the Clinton campaign spending a record-breaking $1.2 billion to securely win the presidency—political newcomer and New York businessman, Donald J. Trump, derailed the entire alt-left revolutionary momentum by explosively winning the 2016 presidential election.

In the hours, days, weeks and months after Donald Trump's huge presidential victory (304 Electoral College votes to Clinton's

228), the alt-left—worldwide—went into complete emotional meltdown which quickly developed into a collective psychological malaise characterized by acute fear, paranoia, anxiety, depression, anger and hatred: labeled by conservative observers as "TDS—Trump Derangement Syndrome."

From Trump's powerful campaign speeches delineating his vision to "Make America Great Again (MAGA)," alt-leftist leaders and those supporting atheistic-socialism soon realized that their secular revolution was now in serious jeopardy. In the White House was everything they professed to hate—a wealthy, conservative, White, Christian male!

Moreover, Trump's vision for America was entirely contrary to atheistic-socialism: (1) instead of global homogeneity, this new president favours strong national sovereignty, legal immigration, enforced border control and a strong military; (2) instead of an entirely secularist society, this new president is intent on defending religious freedom and Judeo-Christian values and culture (such as pro-life, pro-marriage and pro-family); (3) instead of continuing to centralize authoritarian State control in Washington D.C., this new president has promised the American voter to "drain the swamp" of federal government corruption, to wrest economic power from the corporate and media elites, and to wrest political control from the self-serving Democratic and Republican establishments —thereby returning democratic power back to the American people.

Not surprisingly, then, the alt-left and their pervasive zealots in government, business, media communications, academia, psychiatry, intelligence agencies and movie industries have collectively declared war on Donald J. Trump. While radical-socialism publicly professes to promote tolerance, inclusion, diversity, political-correctness, minority rights and respect for others, the alt-left revolutionaries are hypocritically intent on destroying President Trump by whatever means available: Soros-funded riots, fake news reports, FBI surveillance, kangaroo-court challenges, drummed-up impeachment—even public outcries of assassination!

Since atheistic-socialism ideologically rejects divine moral-inspiration, divine good-counsel and divine wise-direction, it instead zealously strives to replace the ultimate moral authority of the one true God with the authoritarian and despotic control of a centralized State bureaucracy. In consequence, alt-left activist groups and political parties (either knowingly or unknowingly) play into the hands of unscrupulous billionaire globalists, such as George Soros, whose corrupt political agenda is to weaken America in order to covertly establish an elitist-controlled, one-world government—historically termed the "New World Order."

President Trump, then, as the peoples' representative of "middle America" (not the leftist corporate, intellectual and media elites in New York, Washington and California) has deliberately, knowingly and sacrificially taken on the stupendous task of resisting, opposing, undoing and defeating the domestic and international forces of the New World Order.

Moreover, on an even deeper and more universal level, since the atheistic alt-left has declared war on Christian persons, groups, beliefs, history, institutions and traditional values it is not just a cultural war that has been sweeping somnolent Western society during recent times; it is obviously a fierce spiritual battle as well. As such, the alt-left revolutionary "movement" unconsciously plays into the diabolical hands of dark spiritual beings, particularly the Antichrist, who are also intent on destroying Christianity and establishing their own evil world-domination and global-control in the near future.

Donald Trump, then, as the presidential defender of religious freedom and Judeo-Christian culture (in America and abroad) at this critical time in world history is clearly a "warrior of light," pre-destined by advanced spiritual forces to help bring America (and by extension, the rest of the world) back to the one true God of love. And while Donald Trump, as American president, clearly occupies a central role in this spiritual struggle, true victory over time will only be achieved when the vast majority of decent, honest, ethical, caring, religious, truthful and peace-loving citizens around the world rise up in unison to actively resist atheistic-socialism and the evil architects of the New World Order.

This book is available to order from Amazon.com

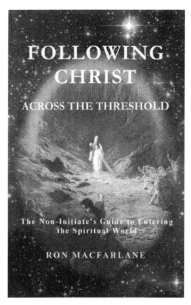

THROUGHOUT the modern age there has been a strong, commonly-held misconception (among religious and non-religious persons alike) that if there truly exists a spiritual world beyond the physical, it is impossible to know anything for certain until after death. And unfortunately (it is believed), no one has come back from death to verify spiritual existence or not. Surprisingly and happily, however, this popular belief turns out to be entirely untrue.

According to esoteric science, mankind has always had the capacity to not only contact the spiritual world *before* death; but on certain rare occasions, the soul is able to exit the physical body *prior to* death, briefly sojourn in the spiritual world and then safely return to the physical body afterwards.

In ancient times, it was only male "initiates"—that is, a small number of specially-selected and carefully-prepared adherents of one of the highly-secretive Mystery Centres in Europe, Asia, the Middle East and North Africa—who were afforded the special opportunity of consciously experiencing the spiritual world while still remaining alive on earth.

Unfortunately, consciously entering the spiritual world in the Mystery Centres involved a hazardous out-of-body procedure made possible by hypnotically placing the initiate into a death-like, comatose condition for three full days. If the initiate successfully revived, all experience and information obtained while sojourning in the spiritual world (termed "gnosis") was secretly kept and closely guarded within the confines of the Mystery

Centre—under the strictest penalty of death.

Fortunately, all this changed with the earthly incarnation of the god-man, Christ-Jesus. Through the transformative power of his own life, death, resurrection and ascension Christ-Jesus forged an entirely new path of secure entry into the spiritual world; as well as a new path of safe return to life on earth. This new Christian path replaced and superseded the dangerous initiatory practices and methods of the ancient Mystery Centres.

Hereafter, those seeking suitable entry into the spiritual world during life (and not simply waiting until death) had two legitimate initiatory paths made available by Christ-Jesus: (1) the path of Mystic-Christianity, and (2) the path of Rosicrucian-Christianity. Both initiatory paths were established though St. John the evangelist (not the apostle).

The path of Mystic-Christianity focuses primarily on affective-emotional spirit-development, using the Gospel of John as the meditative guidebook. Moreover, this initiatory path has been specifically formulated for the stream of *exoteric* Christianity (the Church of St. Peter); and has been commonly practiced within the various monastic orders for hundreds of years.

The path of Rosicrucian-Christianity focuses primarily on cognitive-intellectual spirit-development, using the techniques established during medieval times by the authentic Rosicrucian Order of adepts. This initiatory path has been specifically formulated for the stream of *esoteric* Christianity, and for hundreds of years was secretly practiced exclusively within the hidden confines of Rosicrucian schools. Beginning in the early 1900s, however, a great deal of information regarding the Rosicrucian path of initiation was publicly revealed for the first time by eminent esotericist and initiate, Rudolf Steiner (1861–1925).

What many esotericists are unaware of at the present time is that there exists a third avenue of conscious entry into the spiritual world made available by Christ-Jesus—specifically offered to non-initiates. This unique path has been made possible because of two profound superphysical developments: (1) since his world-altering ascension into the heavenly realm, Christ-Jesus has become the new "lord of karma" governing human evolutionary destiny; and (2) for the past two thousand years Christ-Jesus has been slowly raising the vibratory level within mankind's collective subconsciousness.

As a result, a relatively small number of present-day individuals—with no current initiatory training—have spontaneously experienced brief moments of supersensible perception. To some, Christ-Jesus has fleetingly appeared in his etheric, angel-like resurrection form; while to others he has been perceived as an internal, all-wise spirit-voice. And on even rarer occasions, Christ-Jesus—acting as spirit-guide (or "hierophant")—has consciously escorted non-initiates into the spiritual world for a brief sojourn while still alive, and then safely returned them to physical life on earth.

In all these instances of unexpected and unplanned spiritual encounters, there is a strong karmic (destiny) component involved. Though the individuals involved may not have knowingly undertaken initiatory training in their present lifetimes, in most cases their inner souls were sufficiently prepared in previous lifetimes to enable these extraordinary experiences to occur. Moreover, Christ-Jesus—as the new lord of karma—has the power and authority to grant special dispensation to non-initiates whom he considers worthy of receiving extraordinary spiritual development.

This publication—*Following Christ Across the Threshold: The Non-Initiate's Guide to Entering the Spiritual World*—is not, therefore, a manual of initiatory training. But rather, it is intended as a step-by-step preparatory guide (in the form of a sequential series of "lessons") for non-initiates; in order to assist them as to "what to expect, how to react and what to do" if they are ever granted the opportunity—while still being physically alive—of entering the spiritual world under the inner direction of Christ-Jesus. Hopefully, this intellectual preparation will help alleviate some of the horrific, terrifying and soul-shattering experiences associated with consciously crossing the threshold into the spiritual world during life (and also after death).

Also worth noting for the sincere spiritual seeker, this guide is not a fabricated or theoretical discourse; but is based on profound first-hand experience, since this author—as a non-initiate in his twenty-first year of life—successfully followed Christ-Jesus across the threshold into the spiritual world, and then voluntarily assented to return to physical life in order to share this experience with others. "Thus you will know them by their fruits" (Matt 7:20).

This book is available to order from Amazon.com

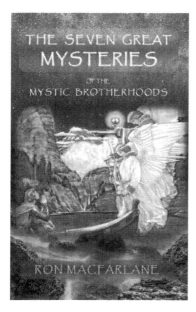

AS FAR BACK AS 1906, in a lecture entitled "Redemption and Liberation," Austrian philosopher and esotericist Rudolf Steiner (1861–1925) indicated that there have been seven extraordinary mysteries of life that have been secretly guarded and exclusively preserved by the Mystic Brotherhoods throughout the centuries. He also indicated that for the first time in history—beginning with the twentieth century—these especial, preeminent life-mysteries are able to be publicly revealed, elaborated, explained and clarified. In Steiner's own words:

There are seven mysteries of life which up till now have never been spoken of outside the ranks of Occult Brotherhoods. Only in our age is it possible to speak of them openly. They have been called the seven "inexpressible" or "unutterable" mysteries … These mysteries are as follows:

1. The mystery of the Abyss.
2. The mystery of Number (which can be studied in Pythagorean philosophy).
3. The mystery of Alchemy (We can learn something of this mystery in the works of Paracelsus and Jacob Boehme.)
4. The mystery of Death.
5. The mystery of Evil (to which reference is made in the Apocalypse).
6. The mystery of the Word, of the Logos.
7. The mystery of Divine Bliss. (This mystery is the most occult.)

Since Rudolf Steiner was himself a highly-advanced initiate and eminent associate of the true Rosicrucian Fraternity, he was obviously familiar with the seven "unutterable" mysteries of the Mystic Brotherhoods and their secret history. During his own lifetime, Steiner was able to reveal a great deal of previously-hidden wisdom regarding the seven life-mysteries. Unfortunately, due to his untimely death at sixty-four years of age, Rudolf Steiner was only able to briefly touch on some of these mysteries; particularly the Abyss, the Logos-Word and Divine Bliss.

Since ancient, pre-recorded times—now obscured by the vast stretch of human history—there have always existed sacred centres of advanced spiritual knowledge and wisdom. These learning centres, later known in Graeco-Roman times as "Mystery Schools" (from the Greek *mystai* = initiates), were closely guarded and highly secretive.

As evolving mankind gradually lost the instinctive clairvoyant ability to perceive the spiritual world, the ancient Mystery Schools were temporarily able to retain experiential access to the spiritual world. Unfortunately, over time, even the Mystery Schools lost direct contact with the spiritual world, and were unable to overcome the acute spiritual darkening that threatened the entire evolutionary existence of mankind.

Hence the incarnation of the God-Man, Christ-Jesus, that was critically necessary to overcome the death-dealing spiritual darkness overtaking mankind; and to provide re-access to the heavenly-worlds of existence. In consequence, the need and function of the ancient pagan Mystery Schools were rendered obsolete by the life of Christ-Jesus; and replaced by Christ-centred brotherhoods such as the Knights of the Holy Grail and the Rosicrucian Fraternity.

The seven great life-mysteries were not kept publicly hidden by the Mystic Brotherhoods for hundreds of years because of selfish possession, elitist privilege, or clannish ownership. Instead, it was because humanity as a whole hadn't undergone the profound spiritual preparations that were crucially necessary to intellectually access and comprehend such deeply-supernal spirit-wisdom.

Thankfully at the present time, despite the widespread hindrances of atheism, secularism and materialism, the intellectual access to the spiritual world is the greatest it has ever been in human history. The profound, intellectually-comprehendible spirit-information contained in *The Seven Great Mysteries of the Mystic Brotherhoods* should be ample testament to this celebratory truth.

This book is available to order from Amazon.com

Also check out the authour's website:

www.heartofshambhala.com

A Site Dedicated to True Esoteric Christianity

Printed in Great Britain
by Amazon

54484139R00106